Summer Steelhead
FISHING TECHNIQUES

Scott Ha...

Dedication

Scott Haugen and his 2-year-old son, Braxton. It was at this age the author's father took him on steelhead fishing trips, planting the seed so deeply in his fishing soul.

This book is dedicated to my son, Braxton. It is my fondest hope that we will spend as many quality days on the river chasing summer steelhead as your grandpa and I have.

The world of fishing allows us to enter realms of nature we may otherwise never venture into. It opens doors of opportunity, provides experiences to last a lifetime and above all else, brings us closer to nature and its Creator.

May you endeavor to pursue and enjoy steelhead fishing to the extent your great-grandfathers, grandfathers and I have. Here's to eternal memories.

Love, Dad

Summer Steelhead
FISHING TECHNIQUES

Scott Haugen

Frank Amato
PORTLAND

About The Author

Scott Haugen was born and raised on Oregon's McKenzie River. At the age of four he hooked and landed his first limit of summer steelhead. His passion for fishing has not waned.

Having traveled and seen much of the world, Haugen cherishes his boyhood home setting most of all. The author, his wife Tiffany and two sons Braxton and Kazden currently reside in the foothills of the Cascades, within sight of the beloved McKenzie River.

Haugen's fervor for the outdoors leads him afield some 200 days a year, be it hunting, fishing or photographing wildlife. A contributor to more than 40 magazines worldwide, Haugen has also written five books and scribed for others. A former high school science teacher and coach, Scott Haugen enjoys sharing his outdoor experiences and educating readers on what he's learned.

One day, Haugen will likely return to the classroom, but until then, you'll find him along the river, in the woods, or partaking in his most cherished pastime, spending time with his family at their Oregon home.

Published in 2003 by
Frank Amato Publications, Inc.
PO Box 82112 • Portland, Oregon 97282 • (503) 653-8108
Softbound ISBN: 1-57188-295-2 • Softbound UPC: 0-81127-00125-5
Photography by Scott Haugen
Artwork by Tony Appert
Book Design: Jerry Hutchinson
Printed in Singapore
1 2 3 4 5 6 7 8 9 10

Contents

Acknowledgements

There are many people who were instrumental in the crafting of this book, some knowingly, others by chance. I would like to thank the many people who assisted in the creation of this work.

From hatchery managers to state biologists, your efforts and insight are much appreciated. Without your dedication to managing such a valued natural resource, this book would not have come to fruition.

Wildlife biologists are to be thanked for their efforts in providing some outstanding summer steelhead fisheries.

To the many anglers I fished with while growing up. Little did we realize at the time, the extent to which the rich knowledge base you fostered within me would grow, allowing me the prestige of fishing and writing for a living. This dream would not have become reality were it not for the influence all of you had on me during my formative years.

For the friends who assisted in gathering information and the all-important photos for this book; I am indebted to you for your efforts. There are also a few strangers out there who assisted when my hands were full, and I appreciate the help. Such is the nature of the summer steelheader. I would also like to thank Tony Appert for his always outstanding illustrations.

I would especially like to thank my dad, Jerry Haugen, the best steelhead fisherman I know. Without his guidance and wisdom, both on and off the river throughout my entire life, I would not be where I am today. He's taught me more about fishing than any single source, and his contagious enthusiasm still gets me excited to wake up early and hit the river.

When she's not editing his work or tending their two sons, the author's wife, Tiffany Haugen, finds time to get out on the river.

Ultimate thanks and appreciation goes to my beloved wife, Tiffany. Though our second son, Kazden, was born a few precious weeks before I typed the final words of this book, she was always encouraging me to push forward, putting my needs above hers. It's her positive support that kept me going, seeing this project through to the end.

Finally, to anyone who has ever caught a summer steelhead, or who yearns to do so. It's you that inspires me to share through the written word, and without your interest, my motivation would be lacking.

Summer steelhead returning to hatchery ponds greatly enhance the number of fish in our rivers and are responsible for getting more anglers on the water.

Introduction

Jvividly recall when I first waded into the North Umpqua River in search of summer steelhead. Though I was only four years of age, I'd been with Dad on this river many times prior, but only as a passive observer. Catching minnows, splashing waterstriders and poking beneath rocks for crawfish proved ample amusement; until I asked Dad when I could start trying for big fish.

I'd caught several trout by this point in my life, but was intrigued by the steelhead Dad kept catching. The night before our big outing, Dad made it a point to optimize the moments of preparation. Together we spooled reels with fresh line, affixed our terminal gear and put all our tackle in order. Little did Dad realize, but those times he spent with me left an impression indelibly etched within my fishing soul.

Awaking at 3:00 a.m. for the two hour journey, the night couldn't pass swiftly enough. Seeing and hearing the rapids of this gorgeous river, smelling the sweet essence of surrounding foliage and making that first cast with the intent of catching a steelhead still hold clear in my mind. Life jacket secure, I edged across the bedrock, knee-deep in the river. Pushing it one step further, I slipped and fell. Soaking my backside, I don't know what scared me more, Dad's reaction or the cold sensation.

After a bit of consoling from Dad, I tried it again. Minutes later I latched into my first summer steelhead. Admiring the nine pound, chrome-bright fish was more than I even anticipated. A few casts later, I had my second steelie. Life couldn't get any better.

That first limit of steelhead came in 1968, and I don't know how many I've caught since then. From California to Alaska, I've been fortunate to pursue summer steelhead along the Pacific Coast. My preferred meeting place with these fish is in upper, fast-moving rivers and streams. It is these waters on which this book will focus.

The author at age four with his first solo summer steelhead taken on Oregon's North Umpqua River.

While I don't consider myself an expert at the sport, I have a deep passion for steelhead fishing and a desire to share what I know. What I've learned over the years has come, in part, from other anglers, relatives and fishing partners, but most of how I fish and what I do has precipitated through my own trial and error.

There are numerous books out there dealing with the specifics behind summer steelhead fishing, but few address the comprehensive, how-to aspects of the sport. In fact, some of the chapters found within this text have entire books devoted to those respective topics. What you'll find within these pages is enough to get you started in the sport on a holistic level, or expand what may be an already solid knowledge base. That said, the ultimate creation of this book was spurred on by steelhead and anglers.

*A clipped adipose fin denotes this as a hatchery fish,
something many steelhead fans are happy to see.*

With successful hatchery programs taking root throughout steelhead waters across the country, annual returns are at all-time highs in many river systems. At the same time, Pacific Ocean conditions have once again turned in favor of the fish, providing nutritious food and favorable survival circumstances.

Because hatchery programs are prospering and the Pacific Ocean's environment is thriving, more anglers are taking to rivers in search of summer steelhead than ever before. Many of these fishermen are learning how to fish for steelhead on their own. During the numerous days I spend on the river, I often cross paths with eager anglers, and field questions relating to the sport.

Sharing what works for me is something I enjoy, and with more anglers taking up the sport, I'd rather see them finding success sooner than later. The earlier in one's fishing career success is had, the more likely a passion will develop for that sport; and that's what we are in need of, anglers who love fishing and enjoy being on the river. It's these anglers who will pass on their affection of the sport to younger generations, and it's the hands of these younger participants wherein the future of sport fishing lies.

First and foremost, successful summer steelhead fishing begins with proper river etiquette. Rivers belong to all of us, and we have to share their bountiful resources. From picking up our own trash, to respecting private property signs, to yielding to other anglers, it must be understood that the days of hitting the river and having it all to yourself are, for the most part, gone.

Nothing turns me off more than to fish near anglers who think they "own the river." Be they guides who make a living from it, or recreational users like myself, the bottom line is, the river is a publicly accessible piece of real estate for all to enjoy. Keep this in mind when you find someone in "your hole" or when cars are parked in "your spot" along the river. There is always other water to be fished and more fish to be caught; don't spoil a fellow angler's time on the river by acting unethically.

Another pet peeve of summer steelhead fishing is when I find lush banks littered with cans, styrofoam containers and fishing line. Not only is this a terrible eyesore—greatly tainting the overall aesthetic experience so unique to fishing this time of year—but it's an environmental disaster. We need not provide such easy ammunition for antifishing groups to key in on with the hope of putting an end to our sport.

Whether you take to the river by boat or on foot, always adhere to the golden rule: "If you pack it in, pack it out." For those anglers truly dedicated to preserving the future of our sport, take the initiative to clean up after others. Carry a garbage bag on the river and gather a bag full of trash on your way out. My dad taught me this when I was young, and I see more and more people getting involved in this act of

Keeping our rivers clean is a responsibility we all share, and is necessary to preserving the aesthetics of pristine waters.

kindness. It's too bad it has to be done, but until everyone cleans up their own act, a certain number of devout anglers will constantly be called upon to offer assistance.

When all is said and done, fishing for summer steelhead is the ultimate in battling big fish under comfortable elements. Feeling the warmth of hot summer days beating on your back, observing waterfowl feeding along the shore, chicks imprinted to their parents, and seeing the mighty osprey hit the water at breakneck speed and coming up with a meal, are just some of the wonders of nature observed by summer steelhead anglers. These magnificent fish are responsible for getting us afield, for opening doors to nature we'd otherwise pass by.

It is my wish that this book will assist in shaping a lifelong zest for steelhead fishing among beginning anglers. I am also confident that experienced anglers will glean valued information from these pages, points that will enhance their already productive approaches to outwitting summer steelhead.

Pound for pound, the summer steelhead's acrobatic tendencies and desire to shake a hook are rivaled by very few other anadromous fish. Once you get a feel for what summer steelheading is all about, you'll be addicted for life.

A double taken by two happy anglers. This is what summer steelheading is all about.

Chapter 1
Meet the Summer Steelhead

As anglers, gaining a comprehensive understanding of the species we pursue is crucial in developing a working knowledge that better allows us to outwit our prey. Hunters devote a great deal of time getting to know the animals they pursue on foot; just because summer steelhead live an aquatic existence does not mean their entire lifestyle and habits should go unnoticed.

By learning the natural history of steelhead, the various habitats they occupy, and the environmental conditions impacting them, anglers can better prepare themselves to catch more fish. Take the invention of scents, for example. There are many scents now on the market, designed specifically for attracting steelhead. When taking into consideration what many of these scents are designed to mimic, the entire range of what a steelhead encounters throughout its life is represented.

Eyed eggs, indicating fertilization has taken place and new life is beginning

From shrimp oils found in the ocean, to nightcrawler scents found in rivers, to pheromones encountered during adulthood and even area-specific scents relating to smolting waters, these all have one thing in common: An understanding of a steelhead's life cycle.

Steelhead are anadromous fish; they are born in fresh water, migrate to saltwater to feed and grow, then move back into rivers or streams to spawn. A steelhead is simply a rainbow trout that has spent a portion of its life at sea.

The average summer steelhead lays about 3,000 eggs. This number can vary depending on the age and size of the adult fish. For instance, a two-salt fish (one that lived in the ocean two years) may deposit 2,000 eggs, while a three-salt fish may contain 5,000 or more eggs.

February through March and into April are the primary spawning months for summer steelhead. Eggs are deposited in small to medium gravel, where they will develop over the next couple of months. Temperature plays a major role in development. A general rule shared by biologists states, "Fifty days at 50° is the average time it takes for an egg to eye, then another 30 days for the egg to hatch." Of course, this can vary due to water conditions in respective parts of the country.

The survival rate to adulthood for wild steelhead averages about 30 fish for every 3,000 eggs laid, or 1%. For hatchery fish, the survival rate to adulthood jumps to about 1,800, or an amazing 60%. Wild fish normally spend two years in the river before heading downstream to the ocean. Hatchery fish spend a year—sometimes two years, depending on hatchery programs—in holding ponds and a year in the river before swimming to sea.

Why is the survival gap between hatchery and wild fish so wide? Quality food and protection from predators are something hatchery fish receive on a regular basis, unlike those of wild fish. In comparison, at the end of a fry's first year of life within a hatchery, it will measure 6 to 7 inches, about twice that of a wild fry raised in the river during that same time frame. This jump-start of hatchery fish is what accounts for such solid summer steelhead returns.

Upon hatching, alevins, commonly called sac-fry, gradually absorb their yolk and eventually emerge from the gravel

In eight months, this summer steelhead fingerling will be released to begin its life in the wild.

as fry. Within hatcheries, fry growth is maximized during the late summer months, when water temperatures hedge on 60°. At this time, a fry's metabolism is racing, and their feeding becomes ravenous. This is a major advantage hatchery fish have over wild brood.

Hatchery fish are released into the river system in the spring, as fry. While fry, or fingerlings, mature in the river, they acquire distinct markings. Eight to 13 of these parr marks may be present on the fish, between the head and tail. At this stage, the steelhead is referred to as a parr, and can be difficult to distinguish from a rainbow trout. During the end of its second year in the river, the steelhead takes on silvery adult coloration, whereby the parr markings are lost. Behaviors start changing and the desire to migrate kicks in. At this point, the little steelhead is called a smolt.

It's the smolt that migrates downstream into ocean estuaries. Under ideal smolting conditions, river levels run high and murky. High water flows keep fish moving downstream at a rapid pace, and cloudy waters help protect them from predators. The timing of smolting is most critical in attaining optimal adult survival numbers, especially among hatchery stock. Depending on the respective rivers, smolts may have to contend with hydroelectric dam control and power canal shut downs; this is where hatchery managers earn their keep, for they try and coincide the timing of smolting to optimal river conditions. Sometimes this may require coordination with several dams on various tributaries.

Once in the ocean, steelhead will remain there from one to five years, feeding on small fish, crustaceans and insects. During the time when a steelhead enters the ocean, to when it returns to its smolting waters, is when nearly all growth takes place. Prototypically speaking, steelhead that spend two years in the ocean, returning to their parent waters at four years of age, weigh 6 to 11 pounds. But, these two-salt steelhead can vary in size depending on ocean diet, distance traveled upriver, river conditions, and obstacles such as dams and ladders they must contend with, all of which add stress.

The same is true for growth potential among three-salt fish, those steelhead that spend three years in the ocean, returning to natal streams at five years of age. These are the big fish everyone yearns for, ranging from 12 to 20 pounds.

Unlike salmon, not all steelhead die after spawning. A male (buck) may spawn with several females (hens), and as a result more bucks expire than hens. Those that survive to once again swim in the ocean will spend time feeding, replenishing fats and body weight lost during the spawn, storing up for their ensuing migration downstream. Steelhead living this long can return to spawn in successive years, given they are capable of living up to eight years under ideal conditions.

Entering streams as adults during the months of April through August—whereby the summer steelhead gets its name—can vary from

*The author with an exceptional steelhead, the
product of a successful hatchery program.*

region to region, stream to stream. In fact, the entire behavior of steelhead can vary, depending on any number of variables. For instance, some rivers get a run of "half-pounders" every summer, steelhead that have been in the ocean only one year before migrating back to their parent stream. At the same time, some steelhead may adopt a residual lifestyle, whereby they hold in a river for up to four years, while others may head to sea when they are one-year olds.

Oddly enough, some steelhead will become strays, whereby they migrate into a different river from where they were spawned or released. Because steelhead migrate to the ocean as individuals, rather than in schools like salmon, their behaviors can vary for reasons unknown to man.

As their time in fresh water extends, and spawning time draws near, steelhead undergo a striking change in coloration. From silver, their body shifts to a darker hue with more pronounced spotting. A pink to reddish stripe accentuates the side, playing a role in the courting and spawning cycles. Once the spawn concludes, the fish slip back to their silver tinge.

Steelhead are ranked among the top five sport fish in North America, and having spent a lifetime pursing them, I'm still amazed at how much there is to learn. By reading all a person can, referencing fisheries biologists and their latest studies, and of course, spending time on the river, anglers will better understand what summer steelhead are all about, gaining a heightened level of respect for what these fish go through in a lifetime. In the end, with some personal research and a strong desire to satisfy a curiosity for what makes these magnificent fish tick, a more complete summer steelhead angler will mature.

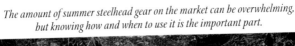

The amount of summer steelhead gear on the market can be overwhelming, but knowing how and when to use it is the important part.

Chapter 2
Reading Steelhead Waters

I once interviewed several guides for a steelhead fishing magazine article. I asked if they'd be willing to share a favorite tactical approach that would help others catch more fish.

One guide responded, "If I share my secrets, I'll lose clients. I can't reveal any tricks I rely on to catch fish." Another guide piped up, "I'll gladly share everything I know." I told the second gentleman about the first man's comment, and asked what he thought. "If you don't know the water, how to read it and where fish lay, all the gear and the most proven tactics in the world won't catch fish." He's right.

No matter what gear your have, how fancy your boat or how decked-out in the latest fishing attire you are, if you don't know what to look for in a steelhead stream, the chances of success remain low. Reading water is the single-most important element for bridging the gap between effort and success.

Keeping in mind that steelhead rivers have unique personalities, be they in Alaska, California or Michigan, they all share common elements steelhead anglers should consider when locating fish. Here, we'll look at what factors impact steelhead and how anglers can use this information to find and recognize the type of waters in which steelhead hold.

Temperature Ranges

Water temperature is one of the most important factors influencing a summer steelhead's behavior, where they will hold in a river, and how active they will be. Dropping a thermometer into the river prior to wetting a line will cut down on the guesswork of where fish will be holding.

Save for Alaskan rivers and a handful of glacial fed streams fished early in the season, water temperatures below 45° are fairly rare when it comes to summer steelhead fishing. But for early-run fish, those showing up in late March, cool waters may be present. In this case—a fish could be anywhere in the river—as water clarity, sky conditions and cool temperatures maximize comfort zones at virtually every depth in the river. Heads of riffles, deep holes, slicks and tailouts are all waters that should be fished.

In water temperatures nearing the 50° point, summer steelhead begin exhibiting a more active lifestyle. They start occupying waters with more chop, moving along seams and holding on breaks. Riffles within the main current also become prime holding spots.

As temperatures rise into the mid-50s, and continue upwards of 60°, summer steelhead reach their zenith in terms of activity. This is when they answer to the widest array of presentations by anglers, and put up the scrappiest of fights. Search for areas with exceptional water flow in which fish will hold. Turbulent waters provide more oxygen and the increased level of surface chop scatters incoming sunlight, making the fish feel safe.

Above 60°, hit shallow riffles in the two- to four-foot depth range. Again, these waters are the most oxygen rich, an element that becomes dangerously low in temperatures of 65° and higher. These riffles also break up solar rays, and help provide a sense of protection, something anglers with quality polarized glasses can capitalize on.

When temperatures reach into the mid-60s, some anglers hang up the rod. At this point, oxygen levels are extremely low and fighting a fish, only to revive it and set it free, will likely result in its death. Unless it's a 100% hatchery run river and you intend on keeping your catch, try to refrain from putting too much unnecessary stress on the fish.

Bottom Types

Different types of river bottoms effect where steelhead travel, and more importantly, hold. One of my favorite steelhead spots throughout the 1970s and '80s produced fish nearly every trip. Then, winter flooding changed things. At first glance, the change was difficult to detect. The same big boulders remained, but amid them, gravel was replaced by sand. Steelhead hate

This boulder patch indicates prime steelhead holding water. Taking the time to fish such locales can pay huge dividends.

sand because not only does it hinder their respiratory system, it also acts as an abrasive on their slime, making them susceptible to disease. Though they are attractive locales, avoid spending time fishing sandy bottoms. Gravel bottoms are where you want to focus your efforts.

Boulder patches and large rocks create ideal steelhead habitat. These obstacles break up current flow, creating areas where fish can hold while conserving valuable energy. The chop, boils and small eddies created by water flowing over and around large rocks are what steelhead search for. It's amazing how, barring structural changes, all fish migrating through such a place will find the same spots, day after day, year after year to hold in.

Depending on time of year, water temperature and clarity, along with sunlight intensity, steelhead may be found in two-foot-deep rock gardens to 20-foot-deep pools strewn with boulders. By considering the following factors, we're getting closer to pinpointing where to fish to hold in.

Sunlight & Water Clarity

The degree to which sunlight penetrates a river has a profound influence on where steelhead travel and hold. Early in the season, when high water conditions are choked with sediments impeding the sun's rays, sunlight cannot penetrate great depths. In this case, concentrate fishing efforts in shallow waters, where light can be maximized to assist in highlighting the presentation. At the same time, in high, cloudy waters, steelhead hit the shallow seams near banks, where less silt passes through their gills and better holding conditions prevail.

Reading a riffle is critical in determining where fish lay, and can greatly boost your success.

As spring progresses and rivers begin to drop and run greenish in color, steelhead feel safe and will begin occupying more shallow sections where tailouts and breaks are present. They'll also hold along rock ledges. Depending upon the type of river, fish may hold anywhere from three to ten feet below the surface in these conditions.

When rivers begin flowing even more clearly, usually coupled with decreased water levels, visibility greatly increases throughout a stream. This means fish are easily spooked, feeling less comfortable in their aquatic domain. As a result, steelhead move to deeper water, where off-color sections provide sanctuary. Deeper riffles, rock walls and gravel bottoms barely recognizable from a human's perspective, will become steelhead holding zones.

Late in the summer—around August in most rivers—water levels are at seasonal lows, flowing clearly. When this happens, steelhead often move into shallow riffles connected to faster sections of water. Search for riffles that are broken, and in particular, those adjoining heavy rapids and powerful chutes. Though the water is low and clear this time of year, the fish are nearly impossible to see when hanging in these waters. But they can really keg-up, especially where chutes significantly drop into riffle-rich waters.

Time of day and sunlight level should also be considered. One of my preferred stretches of river to hit doesn't get what I consider to be good until late in the morning, when the water is caressed by solar rays. Walking into the hole at 10:00 A.M., most anglers are gone, giving me 200 yards of prime water all to myself. Over the course of the next four hours, maximum degrees of sunlight penetrate that hole, forcing the fish into shallow, broken waters. This fast section of holding water leads to a deep, swirling hole, and is topped by deeper, choppy water. Early in the morning, and late in the afternoon, once the sun has left the water, the fish disperse into deeper waters, making them tougher to pinpoint. I've fished several other rivers exhibiting the same type of scenario.

Types of Waters

When it comes to summer steelhead, there is good steelheading water and bad steelheading water. Don't waste your time fishing waters unlikely to harbor fish. Avoid obvious waters like heavy chutes, wide stretches of flat, shallow water less than two feet in depth, and large, deep, swirling holes. Fish may happen into these areas, but they typically won't congregate there.

Because many fast water steelhead streams are carved into mountainous terrain, their gradients are steep and flows rapid. This means that one-quarter to one-third of their waters are fishable. These figures may vary due to river location, surrounding topography, the presence of dams, and the styles of fishing you employ, but it points out that there is a large amount of unfishable water on any given river, despite how good it appears on the surface.

Without a doubt, tailouts are the most recognizable feature on a steelhead stream. Tailouts occur at the bottom of what's usually a good riffle or a deeper section of holding water. Fish can often be spotted and fished to on tailouts, especially when they gather at the shallow, lower end, near the break.

A classic summer steelhead slick where fish often congregate.

An area often overlooked by steelhead anglers are the turbulent waters where a break spills into a riffle. If shelves or large rocks adjoin these waters, steelhead will often nose in here, waiting to make a surge upstream. If you're seeing steelhead on the breaks, hit the fast water seams immediately below them.

Fast flowing water which creates riffles is top steelhead habitat. Riffles are not to be confused with rapids, which occur in deeper sections of the river and move a considerably higher volume of water. Look for chop on the surface, caused by a slow gradient consisting of large rocks and small boulders.

Tom and Michelle Buller nailed this pair of steelhead by swinging sand shrimp over a prime flat spot.

The best steelheading potential exists within these waters. These are the level sections of riverbed that create what's referred to as a holding flat. Because of rock buildup along the bottom, flats may even turn slightly uphill, rather than the typical downstream continuation common to mountainous streams. Flats are loved by steelhead due to the decreased flow of water, which helps them conserve energy.

No matter how you fish steelhead, or in what type of water you're

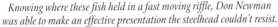
applying the tactics, positioning is an important element leading to success. If you're not correctly positioned on the river, in each and every hole you fish, you won't routinely catch steelhead, no matter what type of tackle you offer. But the key to positioning lies in reading the water.

Only by spending time on the river can you thoroughly develop the skills necessary to catch steelhead, and this goes for learning what waters they inhabit given the wide range of variables that influence their behaviors. By familiarizing oneself with environmental factors, river conditions, and steelhead habits, you'll be able to determine what constitutes prime steelhead water; undoubtedly, this will equate to catching more fish.

Knowing where these fish held in a fast moving riffle, Don Newman was able to make an effective presentation the steelhead couldn't resist.

Chapter 3
Bank Fishing

N ow that you're familiar with summer steelhead behavior and the type of water these fish occupy, you're ready to hit the river. Summer steelhead fishing is popular for several reasons, not the least of which is the ease of accessible fishing waters it offers. However, just because you stand along a river known to hold steelhead, does not mean you'll automatically catch fish.

While the following 15 chapters of this book are dedicated to tactical approaches that will enhance your steelheading arsenal, this chapter is devoted to bank anglers. The largest percentage of summer steelheaders on the river spend time fishing from the bank.

There are several ways to approach bank angling. Perhaps you're out for a day of leisure, where getting away is your primary objective. In this case, the lawn chair and cooler of soda are fine. But to consistently catch fish from the bank, old habits may have to be sacrificed, and new approaches adopted. The ultimate goal is to maximize the time you spend with your line in the water, and this can be done several ways.

Travel Light

Preparing for a trip to the river should start days in advance. While I keep my main gear supply in a Cabela's Advanced Anglers Bag and Flambeau Kwikdraw tackle box, when I hit the river, all of the gear I take fits in a fishing vest, a pair of bait boxes, or somewhere on my person. If hitting varied water, a vest is the way to go, allowing you to apply several strategic presentations. I've had great success with Columbia Sportswear's Henry's Fork II Vest. This allows me to stow lures, Corkies, jigs, bobbers, hooks, baits, flies, a file and any other bit of gear I may need, in one garment. The only item that may need to be carried is a small cooler for bait.

If traveling to the river for a quick morning of fishing, bait boxes strapped around the waist may be the way to go. I like Flambeau's bait boxes due to their large capacity. In one box, fit your sinkers, swivels, drift bobbers, a few lures and any other terminal gear you'll need. In the other box, a baggie or two of cured eggs and a baggie of shrimp can be carried. Your pre-tied hooks can be carried in a Pip's Hook and Leader Dispenser and placed in a pocket. I prefer to carry my fishing license in a small baggie for those times when wading in deep water is necessary, or when I slip and take an unexpected dip. With a rag tied to a belt loop, you're set.

When wading, this is all the gear the author takes, as mobility is the key. A Pips leader box can be kept in the back pocket, while all the sinkers, drift bobbers and bait needed for a day of fishing can be stowed in a bait box strapped around the waist.

Traveling light is the most important element for any bank angler. Being bogged down by hefty tackle boxes, coolers of snacks and beverages, and a long net is the bank angler's worst enemy. In fast water steelheading, few conditions exist where plunking is effective, which means to remain in one place for hours on end may not be the most productive approach. The exception is waiting for steelhead to move through a section of water, where hours can be spent in one spot.

Traveling light, with all the gear on your body, is critical. Doing so allows you to retie without leaving your location. Not only will this save valued time, it will eliminate the likelihood of spooking fish when moving from the water in which you're wading, to the bank and back again.

It pains me to see bank anglers lose a rigging, travel to the shore, retie, and wade back to the fishing, five minutes later. If this is done 12 times a trip`-every time gear is lost, that's a total of one hour of lost fishing time. From the time you break off your terminal gear—to when you get back to fishing again, no more than two minutes should elapse if you're serious about maximizing your fishing time.

By traveling light and being prepared, your fishing time is maximized. If your fishing time is maximized, your catch numbers will increase.

Be Mobile

The lighter you travel, the more likely you are to explore more water. While super magnum tackle boxes are nice, they should be left at home or locked in the truck. At the end of a day's fishing, replenish your vest or bait boxes immediately upon returning home. Take what gear you need from your magnum box, place it in your vest or bait box, and you're ready to go fishing again.

Being tied down by heavy tackle boxes can easily be eliminated, thus permitting greater mobility. If there are vast sections of riverbank to be fished, you're more apt to do so if you are not restricted by cumbersome gear.

Often I'm amazed at what little distance I actually have to travel on a river to have prime sections to myself. The desire to seek out steelhead, rather than await their arrival at a particular section of water, can easily be fulfilled if you're willing to go light and possess the desire to explore new waters. Being mobile also allows anglers to return to places on the river where they know fish will hold, but may not have been present an hour or two earlier. I've done this on numerous occasions, catching fish that had moved into an area while I was gone.

A very successful angler, Russ Mathews moved along the bank to seek out this fish.

At the same time, there's rarely a need to tote a cumbersome net up and down the banks of a river. I've only netted—or attempted to net— one steelhead from the bank my entire life. It was for a friend who hooked it while we were fishing a deep, swirling salmon hole. Though spring chinook were our target, the steelhead nailed his full sand shrimp and Corky. Grabbing the net of an angler near us, the steelhead slipped right through a hole in the bottom and broke off. If, however, you're fishing over a deep ledge or off a steep cut bank, a net may be a safer option than tailing.

Tailing Your Catch

Typically, bank fishing for steelhead is done where shallow sections exist. It's these shallow spots that allow anglers to tail their fish, rather than rely on a net. Again, the less gear you can get by with, the more water you'll cover, and a hefty net is no exception when it comes to dragging it through brush.

Tailing a steelhead is quite simple, it's also easier on the fish if it's going to be released. A thrashing fish in the net loses protective slime, requires more handling, and gets stressed as a result. By playing out a fish, then leading it to shore, it can be worked into a position where you can grab its tail and push it onto the bank, thus the term "tailing." The base of a steelhead's tail is ergonomically shaped to comfortably fit the human hand. This natural fit allows steelhead to be firmly grasped and landed by hand.

When a steelhead gets played out, it will tire and rise to the surface. Working your rod to the side, and simultaneously lifting the tip, will kick the fish on its side, allowing it to glide atop the water as you continue leading it with the rod. Now, lift the rod above your head, being careful not to shortline the fish. Avoid lifting the fish, as placing too much tension on the dead weight of a fish can snap the line and even a rod. You need enough distance between you and the fish to allow yourself to work behind it, while at the same time maintaining a tight line.

With the fish between you and the bank, continue extending your rod tip high over head, keeping the steelhead's nose out of water. Using the momentum of the fish's surge toward shore, bend down and firmly grasp the base of the tail with your free hand. The hand holding the rod will now be positioned behind your back, with the tailing hand in front of you. This position-

Positioning the fish between you and the bank makes tailing easy.

ing ensures a tight line is kept, the fish's head remains up, and provides enough room to attain a firm grasp around the base of the tail.

With the fish firmly in hand, continue sliding it forward, onto the bank. If it's a wild fish or one you choose to release, be sure to keep it in the water during the hook removal stage. Forcing it up on dry rocks causes undo stress, bodily harm and rids the fish of protective slime.

Tailing a steelhead can take practice. You may be inclined to ask another angler to assist, but don't always rely on this as you may one day be alone. In fact, I find it easier to tail my own fish. Due to the fact I'm still holding the rod, I can feel what the fish is doing and predict its next move. Someone chasing it ashore does not have the same connection, and must guess what the fish will do. However you go about it, tailing a fish is surprisingly simple, and the best part, it allows you to cover vast sections of water without being bogged down by a cumbrous net.

Extreme Wading

I can count on one hand the number of times I've worn waders into a summer steelheading river. It's not that I don't appreciate what hip and chest waders have to offer, I do. But I feel the increased mobility afforded by wearing only shorts or good ol' cut-off jeans outweighs the benefits of waders.

Mind you, this is my personal view, and stems from the fact I like covering as much water as I can when bank fishing. When stationary fishing—awaiting steelhead to move to me—I may wear waders, as I'm not walking through heavy brush, blackberries or hiking great distances. When walking, however, I may cover three or more miles a day, and this is best done by wet wading.

Not only can wearing waders get mighty hot while hiking across land to access fishing holes, over time they may rub, bunch up, sweat and just get

plain uncomfortable. Personally, I can only do so much walking in waders, which is why I opt to go without. For my needs, I'd rather wet wade and get a bit cold if it means more comfort over the coarse of a day's fishing.

As for staying dry and warm, heck with that. Don't let trivial issues impede your fishing. Granted, on warm summer days, wading soothes the body, but even early in the season it's not unbearable. Even on those rainy days in May, I'll go without rain pants, wading in jeans or shorts. If I'm going to get wet anyway, be it from rain or the river, I'm not going to sacrifice the benefits of wading over temporarily numbed legs.

Spending an extended period of time where fish are known to gather may be necessary. In this case, finding the most comfortable pair of waders can be the ticket to success, especially in cold rivers.

Seeing the extent to which many anglers go to stay dry directly correlates to the number of fish they catch...or don't catch. Say you're bank fishing with only tennis shoes on, ones you don't want to get wet. If you take the initiative to get wet, wading knee or thigh deep into the river, your angle of presentation dramatically changes, getting you down to where the fish are.

No matter what style of fishing you employ, optimal drifts typically occur the closer you get to where steelhead are holding. The closer you are, the shorter your casts, the shorter the casts, the less drag in your line and the greater the probability of presenting the bait in the steelhead's line of sight. Wading allows you to obtain the ideal casting angle. The more water you can cover, presenting your bait at the optimal angle, the more fish you'll catch, and for my money, this is done by getting wet. Dealing with a cold river is a small consolation to covering as much water as possible.

The freedom of movement wet wading provides is why the author prefers it over all forms of steelhead bank fishing.

Wading Footwear

The style of footwear chosen plays a major part in how much wading will be done. If constantly slipping and falling on slimy rocks, chances are, wading to where you should be won't get done. But fitting the proper footwear to the type of river being fished will change all that.

Matching footware to the type of river you intend on fishing is important for both safety and comfort.

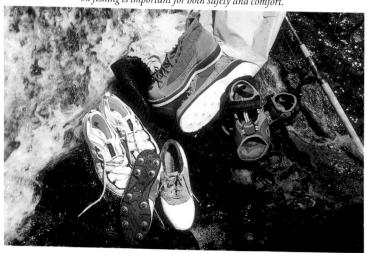

On bedrock river bottoms, I like wearing an old pair of golf shoes. The long metal spikes dig into the soft rock, penetrating the layer of slime that may accrue over the hot summer months. Corkers and metal cleated baseball shoes also suffice.

On rivers mixed with bedrock and boulders, a felt/spiked combo wading shoe may be preferred. The spikes dig into the bedrock, while the felt grabs the rocks. Danner's Studded River Grippers are great for this type of river bottom.

Early in the season-before boulder strewn rivers get covered in slime, or in rivers with a gravel bottom, rubber soled tennis shoes work just fine. If the rocks in these rivers don't acquire slime as the summer progresses, tennis shoes may be worn all season long. Columbia Sportswear makes a variety of such wading shoes with which I've had very good success and comfort. No matter what type of river you fish, the key is matching the shoe to the bottom, and finding a comfortable fit that will allow you to cover a great deal of real estate throughout a day's fishing.

Equipping yourself to travel light is crucial for maximizing bank fishing success. The less unwieldy your gear, the greater the likelihood of covering more water. The same holds true for comfort; the more comfortable you can be, the more of the river you'll be willing to cover. By covering more water, the chance to catch additional fish is optimized, and that's what true bank fishing is all about.

By being properly equipped, the author was able to pull this fish from Alaska's Situk river.

Chapter 4
Spot-N-Stalk Fishing

In early spring when rivers flow full, steelhead move quickly upstream. This time of year fish are seldom seen other than when treading on tailouts or resting in exceptionally shallow waters. As summer months manifest, water levels drop and many fishermen give up pursuing the now skittish fish.

In summer level streams, steelhead have less water in which to rest when migrating to spawning grounds. This is when fishermen can take advantage of natural conditions to improve their odds of catching fish. Many fishermen find steelies too spooked to fish for them at this time of year, for once spotted, the fish often flee or simply will not bite.

I've watched frustrated anglers battle shallow water conditions only to be disappointed when the fish they sought hightailed it for other waters. A common error is beginning the hunt too late. Rather than spotting fish from as far away as possible, I'll sometimes catch myself walking, head down, to stream's edge. By this time it's too late to sneak within sight of any steelhead and still maintain hopes of hooking him. Once you've been detected, the gig is up.

Few summer steelheading experiences are as thrilling as sight-fishing.

*Using quality glasses is the most important factor in spotting steelhead.
Knowing what to look for ranks a high second.*

Where to Start

The search for fish begins with quality, polarized glasses. There are several brands on the market, with a wide-range of price variance. The one that's right for you depends on how much money you are willing to spend. Typically, the more you invest, the better your return is in terms of quality, longevity and overall effectiveness. Whatever brand you purchase, make sure when trying them on there is enough space between your brow and the frame to allow air movement. I've owned some very expensive glasses that lacked this feature and caused fogging on hot, humid days, the time when spotting summer steelhead is at its peak. At the same time, ensure the glasses don't create distortion that will interfere with your ability to spot fish. I've been extremely happy the past couple of years with my Action Optics glasses, as they give me all the comfort and features I need to spot any anadromous fish.

Like hunting wild game, the key to success is spotting steelhead as soon as possible—hopefully before they see you. To do this, tediously search from the brush bordering a riverbed, or seek high ground from which to observe.

Approaching one honey-hole I like to fish, I hike uphill a good 75 yards above the stream and begin surveying. Large rocks are strewn about the riverbed and steelhead battle to maintain their equilibrium where the current is swift and can change. With the sun overhead, it's possible to catch glimpses of silver flashes as steelhead maneuver for position in the river. Once fish are located, anticipation mounts and the fun begins.

If you don't have the luxury of a hillside from which to spy fish from, there are plenty of other high spots that can be utilized to search for holding steelhead. Bridges are good high points to survey from, though such structures may be limited if they are not located over ideal steelhead waters. High rocks or boulders will also give you elevation, and though it might not be as high as you'd like, it's better than standing on flat ground.

Trees are another vantage point that will put you above fish. Be certain to get a sturdy footing when climbing trees and if you are scaling a tree overhanging the water, make sure you are not creating undo movement which may alert fish to your presence. Elevated roadsides can also be a valuable search location from which to spot fish.

The use of a ladder is an approach growing in popularity among anglers. Due to their cumbersome nature, ladders can't be carried long distances along the riverbanks, but if you have one good hole to sight fish, that's all you need. Securing the ladder in the river, anglers stand toward the top, casting to fish as they pass by. I've also observed people parking a truck at water's edge, ascending specially constructed frames in the back, and catching fish. It looks crazy, but it works.

When it comes to seeing steelhead, gaining an elevated vantage point can make all the difference. Standing tall in a boat is one way to achieve the ideal angle. Bank fishermen can also tote a ladder, greatly enhancing their field of view.

What to Look For

Locating steelhead takes practice, for not always can you see their shiny silver sides. With natural light striking the water at different angles throughout the day, their backs vary from brown to blue to greenish in color and spotting them can be as much of a challenge as latching into one.

In shallow water conditions, steelhead often lay behind or in front of large rocks, where current is reduced. They can be difficult to spot in these locations. Also, rippling water creates numerous erratic prisms that refract light, scattering the image of the fish and making it extremely challenging to detect the presence of even the largest steelhead.

Steelhead also take to rippling waters, as the undulating current breaks up direct sunlight. Such places are often overlooked as people believe the water is too shallow to hold fish. By knowing what to look for in terms of reading the water—not necessarily spotting the fish themselves—you can increase your odds of catching fish.

I fished with good friend Bret Stuart one July day and we located more than 30 steelhead holding in a section of rippling water. The water ranged from two- to three-feet deep, yet it was difficult to make out fish. A boat soon drifted by, both anglers eagerly searching for steelhead. Passing us, we asked if they'd seen anything. "Not a fish," was the reply. For some reason, they failed to see a single fish in the entire group as they passed by.

Another shallow water hangout common among steelhead is a natural depression where the current flows over their backs, allowing them to effortlessly rest. These fish are normally easiest to spot, but it's crucial to locate them before they spy you. These holding locations are very clear and often close to shore, so the fish are on the alert for predators at all times.

If you find such a resting place, try making a cast well away from the water's edge. Casting 20 yards away from the waterline is not unreasonable, and will allow you to work your bait in front of the fish without him knowing you are there. The biggest challenge of casting over so much dry real estate to reach the water is the retrieve back over land. It can be frustrating reeling across rocks, sticks and through low-lying bushes which often results in hang-ups, so make your first cast count.

This fish refused a half-dozen baits before attacking a sand shrimp laced with Smelly Jelly.

Perhaps the most common place to hunt steelhead is on tailouts, where they are easy to see through the glass-like water. Where the river necks down and spills into rapids, a slick usually forms, and fish often pull off to the side of these areas to rest. These fish can be uneasy, as they have just as good a view from their aquatic environment as you do into it.

Other Factors to Consider

It takes time on the water to learn how to spot steelhead. If you spook a fish before wetting a line, don't think of it merely as a blown stalk, learn from it. Steelhead are constantly on the move and another fish will eventually seek the same location to hold and rest.

If flooding, changing river courses, or silt don't impede a holding location that you know held fish in the past, head right to those spots the following season. Some of my favorite holding zones have been producing fish for the past 20 years.

Time of day and cloud cover can make a world of difference when it comes to spotting fish. Steelhead are typically easier to locate when the sun's rays shine directly on the water. Once shadows of mountains, clouds, or trees are cast on the surface, the ability to discern fish can be inhibited. There are several sections of various rivers I prefer fishing at midday, when direct sunlight prevails. As a result of increased sunlight penetrating the water, my fish-locating ability noticeably increases. I've hooked most of my fish in these spots at midday, after many fishermen have hung up their rods for the day.

If sight fishing from the bank, you may want to try working a limited stretch of water over the course of the day. Constantly monitor the same holding spots, the ones you know have previously held fish. If you see nothing, continue on, but return repeatedly to check and see if any fish have moved in.

If you are fishing from a driftboat, try working back-and-forth as you move downstream. Don't be hurried to head straight down river, you may pass by several prime holding spots. Anchoring the boat and standing on the seat or the bow will give you valuable elevation and is a great way to spot fish from the middle of a river.

Though striking in color, steelhead can be very difficult to see. Only through repeated practice can the human eye become conditioned as to what to search for.

The Presentation

There are two approaches when casting to fish that have been detected: drifting a bait by them or anchoring it on their nose. In either case, cast well upstream of the resting fish so as not to spook it, all the while anticipating where your bait will end up.

If drifting a bait by steelhead—in hopes he'll grab it on the move—mark where each cast hits the water. This will allow you to make necessary corrections on ensuing casts.

If a fish does not react to a drifting presentation, try securing it on his nose. This is best done by increasing the amount of lead you use. If using a 1/4-ounce sinker to drift by a fish, slap on two or three ounces and try placing the bait an inch or two from his nose. This approach, along with changing baits, say from eggs to nightcrawlers, can be the ticket. At times, such changes seem to irritate fish and can trigger an aggressive attack.

Hunting for steelhead is different from ordinary blind fishing. The excitement of discovering a 15-pound fish and enticing it to take your bait is exhilarating. Once you master the spot-n-stalk approach, you'll wonder how you ever did without it.

Chapter 5
Fine-Tune Your Drift Fishing

As discussed in Chapter 2, reading the water is the most critical element in determining consistent angling success. The best gear in the world is virtually worthless if you don't read the water and have the ability to determine where steelhead will be. But if you know what to look for, and set yourself up accordingly, regular success can be attained.

However, water conditions can vary from river to river, even on one river during the course of a day. A dam may be opened or shut down and water levels will fluctuate accordingly, but that's no reason to stop fishing. By fine-tuning your drift-fishing approach to fit the numerous river conditions, a heightened level of triumph is within grasp.

The Technique

Prior to addressing the many facets of gear that can enhance your drift-fishing arsenal, let's first consider the basic drift-fishing technique. The key is not to fish the heaviest weight you can get away with, without getting hung up, but to fish the lightest weight you can find that barely skims the bottom.

Fishing heavy weight finds your sinker aggressively pounding the bottom. Each time this action pulls your rod tip down, it's also dragging the bait to the bottom, below a fish's line of sight. By periodically ticking the bottom throughout the course of a drift, you're keeping the bait floating higher, where steelhead can see it.

Maneuvering your rod to achieve the proper line tension will also aid in attaining the perfect drift. Lowering the rod tip allows you to feel the bottom while raising it will allow you to detect bites and the tops of larger rocks. Keep slack out of the line, so you can feel what's going on below the surface; if you need to add or subtract weight to achieve this, do so accordingly. The more you practice this approach, the better you'll become.

When setting up to properly drift-fish a section of river, work from the top of the hole, moving downstream. By presenting the bait on the upstream side, you're achieving a natural presentation that won't spook the fish. Haphazard casting into the middle of a hole may land where fish are laying. Avoid spooking them by systematically working your way downstream, from the highest point possible.

At the same time, start working a hole by casting close to where you're standing, and making each successive cast farther away. This will prevent casting over fish that may be near you. A buddy once did this and nailed three nice fish from the same hole; one near his feet, one in the middle of the river and one off the opposite shore. Had he begun by casting in the middle, chances are that a hooked fish would have spooked one of the others.

When drift fishing, break the river down into sections and fish each one as if it were its own entity. I like "gridding" a stretch of water, whereby I make several casts, working my way across the river. I then change my physical position, moving downstream, repeating the same series of casts. It may take a couple of hours to work a single section of water, but it's vital to be thorough when drift fishing, especially if searching for fish.

Water level, flow rate, and turbulence will determine at which angle your casts are to be made. In fast waters, it's typical to make casts upstream at a 45-degree angle or so. This allows the terminal gear to be hitting bottom by the time it's directly in front of you. In slower moving water, casts may be 10° upstream from where you stand. The only way to determine which angle works best is through repeated practice. Eventually, you'll get to the point where you can look at a river, determine its rate of flow, and decide precisely where to cast in order to optimize a drift.

Once you hit fish, make a note of the exact conditions and their location. I'm still picking up fish on the same holes I have fished for over 30 years, and where my grandfathers caught fish 30 years prior to my taking up the sport.

Drift Bobbers

Since the 1950s, drift bobbers have been used to take steelhead. While Yakima Bait Company's Corkies are far and away the most popular drift bobber on the market, there are other brands and styles that can be used to take summer steelhead with regularity. Non-winged bobbers like Beau-Mac's Cheaters and Pills, Luhr Jensen's Okie Drifters and Yakima Bait's Wobble-Glos are all constructed of high-floating material designed with two purposes: to lift the bait, placing it in the steelhead's line of sight, and to add color to attract the attention of fish.

Drift bobbers come in an array of sizes and colors. For Corkies and Cheaters, sizes 14, 12 and 10 are most commonly used on summer run fish, while the smaller size 1 or 2 Okies are also good choices. A size 12 or 10 Wobble-Glo and Pills of size 1 are optimal for summer steelheading conditions. These smaller size drift bobbers are effective in fast water steelheading terrain, where low, clear water is the norm. For added buoyancy or color combinations, stacking two size 14 or 12 Corkies or Cheaters is an effective tool.

In high, silted rivers, larger drift bobbers can be employed, as can the use of winged drift bobbers. Winged bobbers provide more action than do

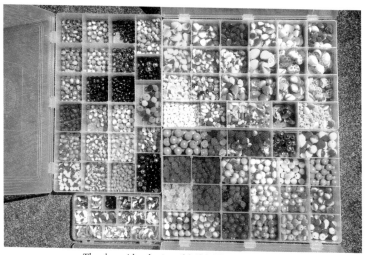

*There's a wide selection of drift bobbers available to
steelheaders; they all have their place in summer fishing.*

those listed above, thus attracting the attention of fish. The action of winged
drift bobbers will also impart a life-like action to shrimp, worms, roe and
crawdad tails, enhancing their level of visibility.

The Spin-N-Glo's soft, white plastic wings and light-reflective Mylar wings
are an added bonus on any fishing rig. Sizes 14, 12 and 10 are most popular for
summer steelhead, while you can go up to a size 8 in murky waters.

Flashing and Spinning Cheaters—Cheaters with wings—were the first
drift bobber to feature Mylar wings. The stiff wings convey unmatched
action and light dispersing capability, both of which are a deadly combination on steelhead. These are excellent choices in high, off-colored water, or
early in the season when water temperatures are low. The added movement
sparks lethargic fish to react, something stationary bobbers might not illicit.

Both the Spin-N-Glo and Flashing and Spinning Cheater should have a
3mm to 4mm bead threaded between them and the hook. Not only does the
bead allow the winged bobbers to freely spin, it prevents yarn from being
twisted into the bottom hole of the bobber.

Though there are numerous color combinations available when it comes
to drift bobbers, the choice of what color to select can depend on water color,
degree of daylight, water temperature, and even personal preference.
Typically, three general shades of drift bobbers are preferred: light, dark, and
pearlescent. For whatever reason, pearl pink draws the most numerous
strikes, no matter what conditions prevail. I know of anglers who use pearl
pink bobbers 90% of the time, and with good success. Dark colors—blacks,

blues, purples, browns, etc.—create a silhouette-type figure when fished in dark conditions. Light and brightly colored bobbers, when fished in bright circumstances, reflect bright hues, capturing a steelhead's attention.

Experiment and take time to see what colors work best for you on the waters you fish. Not only should you tinker with drift bobber colors, but you should explore yarn colors and baits with which these attractants are combined. As you develop confidence in certain styles and colors of drift bobbers, you'll find this assuredness factors into your selection more than any other element.

To increase the visibility of your presentation, try stacking a pair of drift bobbers. This will also add lift to your bait.

Soft Artificials

There are several soft artificial attractants designed for drift fishing. I recall, when I was a young boy in the early 1970s, cutting up my mom's orange sponge she used to wash her car. My egg supply was nil, and the orange sponge soaked in anise oil looked and smelled great—it even caught fish.

Sponge baits can be made by cutting up a synthetic household sponge. Colors and sizes are left to personal preference. Threaded on to your leader with a sewing needle, above a 3mm bead, sponges can be a cheap, quick addition to the arsenal. But remember, sponges absorb water, so they must be squeezed free of river water every few casts. Scents of choice can be added to sponges to enhance their fish-catching ability.

Rags are another homemade type of drift bobber. Cut a 1/2- to 1-inch section of soft foam. Closed-cell foam, like that used in the construction business for installing windows—referred to as backer rod or backer foam—is best, as it retards against water absorption. Thread colored yarn through either 1/2 or 3/4 inch in diameter piece of backer foam, using a heavy duty sewing needle. Leave approximately 3/4 of an inch of yarn hanging out from each side of the foam. (You can add several colors of yarn if you'd like.)

An efficient way to prepare several rags at a time is to cut a few dozen pieces of foam to length, threading them all on a long piece of yarn. At this point, thread through any other yarn colors of choice. All you have to do now is go down the line, cutting the yarn to length. This method beats

Rags are economical, very effective tools for steelhead; they're also fun to create.

hand-threading each individual piece of foam, allowing you to create numerous rags in a short period of time.

Rags are easy to make, cheap, and work well in fast water. Their added buoyancy keeps them riding higher in the water than other drift bobbers, a bonus when working around boulder-strewn bottoms where currents can push the rag around into a steelhead's line of sight. Due to their construction, rag bodies are also ideal for injecting and holding artificial scents.

Though they don't seem to produce to the level of other drift bobbers, soft plastic or rubber artificial baits do have their place in summer steelhead fishing. On rivers where natural baits are banned, these rubber substitutes work well for the simple fact fish are more likely to hold on to them once bitten. The soft bodies resemble real eggs, and many come with built-in scent chambers, for easy injection of artificial scents. Some even have scents incorporated into them, direct from the manufacturer.

Rubber eggs have the benefit of being soft, meaning fish are less likely to spit them out once they've made contact.

Gooey Bobs, Bob Tails, Sac Attacks, Bouncing Eggs, Steelhead Slayers, Jenseneggs and other such designs are readily available. These can be fished on the shank of a hook or atop the eye, like a standard drift bobber. With a bit of yarn added to the presentation, these are very good looking steelhead setups.

Plastic Worms

Plastic, or rubber, worms are nothing new to steelhead fishing, though they are more common in parts of Canada than in the Lower 48. Hand poured worms are arguably the best type, versus the injection molded style. Hand poured worms are softer and have more color possibilities. While the straight tail style is most common, spade and paddle tail designs should not be overlooked. In fast water, all will provide great action, and line twist will be kept to a minimum.

While worm color possibilities are endless, it's the pink and orange worms that capture most steelheader's attention, regardless of water and sky conditions. Earth tones such as brown and black can also be productive and are preferred by some anglers when fishing clear, low water.

With a wide array of plastic worms out there, it's these colors in the two- to four-inch range that most summer steelhead anglers like.

Fished alone or threaded onto a hook beneath a drift bobber, plastic worms create realistic movements, like what you'd expect to see when high water causes erosion along the riverbank, flushing worms into the system. A worm threader can also be used to rig a plastic worm. Slide the worm onto the threader, an inch or so above the tail end. The threader will exit the head end. Now slide the entire worm over the eye of the hook, onto the leader, with the section of tail dangling freely. This method creates a natural presentation steelhead will attack.

Worms in the two- to four-inch range are most common, though six-inch worms can be used with success in low visibility conditions. Plastic worms are fished like any other bait when drift fishing and are ideal when searching for steelhead.

Smile Blades

Mack's Lures has a Smile Blade which has remained a secret to many steelhead anglers. Placed atop a pair of 3mm beads, this plastic blade produces a gyrating, wiggling action that stimulates fish to bite. The vibrant mylar blade gives off a 360° angle of light reflection that captures the attention of fish from afar.

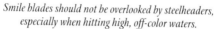
Available in three sizes, it's the smallest version that works well on fast water metalheads. Fished alone or in combination with bait—just as you would fish a standard drift bobber—the Smile Blade works great in all water conditions. Due to its sensitivity, it's particularly effective in slow stretches of the river and in turbid settings.

Smile blades should not be overlooked by steelheaders,
especially when hitting high, off-color waters.

Sinker Setups

Several varieties of sinker setups are used in fast water steelheading, but they can be narrowed down to a few that prove very effective. Bank sinkers tied to a dropper are good when plunking, but very little of this method can be applied in fast, shallow summer run streams.

More typically, sinkers are set up for drift fishing, and as such, pencil lead and slinky sinkers steal the show. These two sinker systems meet most, if not all, fast water steelheading needs. The Bouncing Betty is popular among drifters, and does well where bouncing gear along the bottom is desired.

Slinky sinkers have been around for years, and continue to grow in popularity. Because the slinky sinker carries with it a snagless feature, it's great for those learning a new river or for exploring unfamiliar bottoms. The nylon cord covering of the slinky glides over rocks, not sticking to them like lead will. This accounts for a smoother drift, far fewer hangups, and less loss of gear.

Some argue they don't like the sensitivity lost when using slinky sinkers; others say they like the increased level of sensitivity. As with many aspects of drift fishing, it boils down to personal preference.

By clipping slinky sinkers to a snap swivel, they can be rigged to slide along the mainline, or they can be snapped to a barrel swivel to which the leader and mainline are tied. Either way, both styles are great for summer steelhead. Where summer fish occupy shallow, clear water, slinky sinkers are prime for tantalizing presentations. Slinkies move at the perfect rate for fishing fast water—a bit slower than the current flow itself, yet faster than what lead moves. In summer, when water temperatures are in the mid-50s, a steelhead's metabolism is considerably faster than when the water is cooler. The faster drift afforded by slinkies is perfect in such conditions, where fish react more aggressively.

Slinky Sinkers can be clipped into your barrel swivel (top). making it stationary, or be free to slide along the mainline (bottom).

As for the size of slinky to use, that can only be determined through trial and error. Make up several slinkies of various sizes prior to hitting the river, both from small and large shot. Once on the river, you can adjust to the desired size. It's better to start with slinkies that are too heavy, versus too light. With heavy sinkers, the cord can be cut, shot removed, and with a small lighter, sealed back up. That quickly, you're back to fishing.

If the water is cooler, or the flow is rapid, you'll need to slow the presentation down. This is best done with lead. Pencil lead—be it cast from molds or bought in hollow-core spools—sticks to rocks, slowing a presentation. The feel of lead hitting the bottom is decidedly sharper than that of a slinky, and more gear will be lost. But there are many devout pencil lead anglers who won't convert to anything else, convinced this is the best sinker system going. Much of their argument centers around the lead being more sensitive, quicker to replace, and its ability to sink more rapidly after a cast is made.

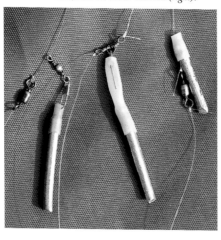

Pencil sinkers and surgical tubing create an ideal sinker system. They can be free to move along the mainline (left) or be stapled into a three-way swivel and fished stationary (middle). The rubber tubing can also be slid onto the mainline, and the sinker inserted (right).

Pencil sinkers can be rigged to a snap swivel holding rubber tubing, or inserted into a piece of rubber tubing which will allow them to firmly slide along the mainline. They can also be fixed to a three-way swivel with the tubing stapled in place, or in the case of hollow core lead, clamped on to the tag end of the mainline.

Only through time on the river can you decide which sinker system best suits your fishing needs. The more you fish, the more you'll develop confidence in your gear, and hopefully discover that both sinker systems are valuable steelheading tools.

Proper Line

With a plethora of lines on the market, I'm not going to get into evaluating one brand versus another. But line weight is an issue that must be addressed. There are two schools of thought when it comes to summer steelhead fishing: Go with light line to avoid being detected in clear water conditions, or go with heavy line to hold the fish.

Anyone who has fished popular holes, and repeatedly been hung up on broken lines littering the bottom, frowns on those who use light line. Nothing ruins a good fishing hole faster than having it choked with endless yards of fishing line, a result of anglers hanging up and breaking off.

As far as I'm concerned, there's only one choice of line when it comes to holding steelhead with a baitcasting setup: heavy. Early in the season, when rivers are high, 12-pound mainline is a minimum, accompanied by 10-pound leader, but some people use 15- and 17-pound mainlines for their increased holding power. As water levels drop, the lightest mainline I'll go to is a 10 pound with an 8-pound fluorocarbon leader. Due to their structure and ability to displace pressure when fighting a fish, longer spinning rods and quality reels afford the use of considerably lighter gear; going down to a 6-pound mainline and 4-pound leader is within reason when in the hands of experienced anglers.

However, in my book, fishing fast water with 8- and 6-pound mainlines, and 6- and 4-pound leaders are not doing the fish justice. It's simply too difficult holding fish with such light line. The argument by anglers using such line centers around lighter weights being less visible. Though this used to be the case, it's still not viable when it comes to breaking off more fish than necessary. Additionally, the advent of fluorocarbons has changed things. This tough, quality product with its reflective index nearly identical to water, makes for an invisible line that will not be detected by even the wariest of fish, meaning anglers can use a strong, larger diameter line with low visibility.

When you do get hung up, there is a right and a wrong way to break off your terminal gear. The wrong way is to grab the reel with your hand and start walking up the bank. This puts the stretch and tension on the line right at the spool, which is where the resulting break usually occurs. Instead, make three or four raps of the line around your forearm, between the reel and the first guide. Grab your rod with the same hand around which the line is wrapped, point the rod tip directly at the hangup site, and walk up the bank, or pull straight against the hangup if fishing from a boat. Your arm will absorb the stress, placing the highest tension on the terminal gear. As a result, the gear will break off at the swivel, leaving only your terminal gear behind, not 30 yards of unwanted line.

Line should be changed after every three or four trips. After fishing rivers with many ledges, or dragging over bedrock strewn systems, I'll change line at the end of each day of fishing. Frayed line can be easily replaced, and doing so increases the probability of landing fish. It also prevents fish from swimming around with several yards of line dangling from their mouths.

Leader Length

In summer stream conditions, leader length is critical for success. While leader length restrictions apply on many rivers and in many states, the shorter leader length you use, typically, the better. The purpose is to get the bait in front of the fish as quickly as possible, and in shallow, fast moving water, this is best done with a short leader. A 12-inch leader is not unreasonable in tiny tributaries.

A quality fluorocarbon leader is important, especially in clear streams. The properties of this material allow you to stay with a stronger leader, rather than settling for a small-diameter, weaker line.

In larger rivers running very clear, leaders in the 18- to 36-inch range are good. These longer leaders are necessary for separating the sinker from the bait, so as not to spook the fish.

Extremely long leaders also have their place. Eight to ten-foot leaders can be effective in clear, shallow water, where a natural presentation is desired. With the weight so far removed from the bait, the sinker still serves the purpose of slowing the rate at which the bait moves downstream. At the same time, the bait is left to float about more naturally. A buddy watched a guy next to him land 19 summer steelhead from a single spot on the river one morning using an 11-foot leader. In the right conditions, long leaders do have a place.

Rods & Reels

Rods and reels used in summer fishing are up to the individual angler, and there are as many variations as there are fishermen. Basic, fiberglass spinning rods serve the purpose, as do the highest quality graphite rods and baitcasting reels money can buy.

Having fished with a multitude of rod and reel combinations, if I had one all-around drifting fishing setup to choose from it would be an 8 1/2-foot graphite rod equipped with a smooth baitcasting reel. The sensitivity afforded by

In the author's opinion, the reels on the left are the two best ever created for steelheading. Unfortunately the Shimano 201 and 251 are no longer made, but the Cabela's Black Label II reel with its flipping mechanism will get the job done in most situations.

graphite allows you to feel every tick of the bottom, ultimately resulting in a more thorough comprehension of what constitutes the waters you fish. The more you know about the river, the better your odds of catching fish, and a quality rod can make a big difference.

A quality baitcasting reel is also crucial. Baitcasting—or levelwind reels—allow you to work terminal gear to where you want it. Quickfire free spool reels and flipping style reels work well on steelhead streams, optimizing casting efficiency. They also allocate room for freespooling or backing terminal gear downstream toward the end of a drift. This style allows you to drop the bait where you want it, ultimately covering more water and discretely placing it where a fish my be lurking.

Of course, the best way to maximize your drift fishing acuity is by spending time on the river. Observing successful anglers and studying what they do to catch fish is a good way to learn the art of steelhead fishing. However, deciphering the difference between rocks, trout and steelhead bites can only be learned through personal experience. These are occurrences that are impossible to relate on paper. But that's what is so special about summer steelheading; there are lots of fish available, and learning develop rapidly. By maintaining an open mind and being persistent in your efforts, you'll become a seasoned student of the sport before you know it.

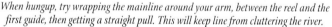

When hungup, try wrapping the mainline around your arm, between the reel and the first guide, then getting a straight pull. This will keep line from cluttering the river.

Chapter 6
Gettin' Jiggy With It

Jig fishing for steelhead is nothing new to western steelhead anglers, but the way Oregon guide Bret Stuart approaches it is. Stuart, owner and operator of 24/7 Guide Service, has it down to a science, and what I've learned from him the past few years and what I've picked up through my own trial and error have added a new and exciting dimension to the way I attack steelhead.

The setup is easy and inexpensive, depending on how elaborate you choose to go on the rod. I've used everything from a low-cost, glass spinning rod to a 12-foot graphite noodle rod. The longer rod is preferred as it gives greater flexibility in terms of accessing more fishing water, but that nine-foot spinning rod can be made to work just fine.

When initially trying jig fishing, I made the mistake of going with my baitcasting setup. I didn't even realize I was doing it all wrong. I love rolling eggs for steelies, and carting another rod setup around just to fish with jigs seemed unnecessary. "Why not carry the bobber and jigs in my pocket and not worry about fumbling with another rod," I thought. After two days of dedicated fishing with bobbers, and not getting so much as a single nibble, I reverted to my usual tactics and wrote jig fishing off as a fad. Not until I personally fished with Stuart did I learn how to properly work a bobber and jig.

The spinning outfit is the most critical element in jig fishing. Without it you won't cover water, you can't properly work the bobber, and the jig will not be fished with 100% accuracy. A spinning reel lets you position the jig where you want it and allows you to more easily mend the line when needed, which can be several times a cast in fast water. This is something that simply cannot be done as effectively with a baitcasting arrangement.

Guide Bret Stuart, creator of the Stuart Steelhead Bullet, with one of hundreds of fish he's taken on his popular jig.

The second key element in jig fishing is the bobber stop. This little device forever changed the art of jig fishing in fast water, opening up many avenues for steelhead anglers to explore.

The entire setup consists of a jig tied to a leader, the opposite end of which is tied off to a size 7 barrel swivel. Above the swivel, on the mainline, sits the bobber and above that a small bead. Affixed to the line above the bead, is the bobber stop—a piece of string which snugs against the line, not moving until you make it. Rod wrapping string or a heavy gauge thread works best, as it will not slide up and down the line until you physically move it. You can purchase pre-made bobber stops, complete with beads, which work great. The function of positioning the bead between the bobber and stop is to prevent the stop from passing through the bobber.

If using the commercial bobber stop, the tube around which it is tied will be the first item threaded on your mainline. Once on the line, simply slip the nylon knot off the tube, cinching it snugly on your line. Remove the tube from the line, thread your bead, then bobber, and you're set. Below that will be the barrel swivel and jig.

By positioning the bobber stop where you want it, you control the depth at which you fish. If you want to fish in a foot of water, simply shorten the leader to six to eight inches and slide the stop down near the top of the bobber. If you want to fish 20 feet of water, slide the stop 20 feet up your line.

The beauty of the bobber stop is that it easily winds on the spool and slides freely through the guides when cast. This allows you to fish bobbers in deep water, as casting with an extended leader is no longer a concern. The bobber stop allows for any and all steelhead water to be

The ideal jig setup: A bobber stop fixed to Fireline mainline, followed by a bead and the bobber. Below the swivel is the leader and jig. The depth at which you fish is determined by the bobber stop, and can range from one to twenty feet as the stop slides freely through the guides when cast.

fished. An added bonus of fishing with bobber and jig is that it yields very few hang ups, keeping you fishing.

The first time I properly fished jigs, I was amazed at how much water I covered. Though I'd fished the same section of river for a quarter-century, it seemed like a foreign body of water. The jig setup allowed me to fish stretches of river I normally passed up...and I caught fish.

I anchored in my favorite riffles and casted upstream, letting the jig float freely down. But what changed was the angle at which I fished. In drift fishing, casting too far upstream means hang ups, and finishing off the drift way downstream will result in fast water forcing your terminal gear to the surface. With the bobber, there's no concern of hanging up by casting too far upstream or not fishing water by letting it drift too far down.

Jig fishing is designed to make fish attack. Steelhead are predators, and even in mountain streams they will aggressively feed, be it out of hunger or instinct. If the jig can be presented within a 97° degree window, or directly in front of the fish's nose, steelhead will be more inclined to come up and strike. Presentation is a key element to success in jig fishing and reaching this position is critical if you want to catch fish. Since jigs are weighted, 1/32 to 1/4 ounce are preferred for summer fishing activity, they must be kept off the bottom, in the fish's line of sight. This is where a good bobber is a must.

It's crucial to create a balance between bobber and jig. If fishing a 1/16 ounce jig, use a small profile, 1/16-ounce bobber. If changing to a 1/8-or 1/4-ounce jig, use a 1/8-or 1/4-ounce bobber. The two types of bobbers I prefer are a foam bobber crafted by West Coast Floats and the wooden, Center Slide bobber created by Thill. Both work great for they are streamlined, sensitive, offer high visibility, and are easy to read. The smaller, more intricately designed the bobber, the less likely fish are to detect any resistance when striking the jig. Additionally, these floats allow the jig to move downstream in a natural position. Large bobbers tend to be carried ahead of the jig in fast water, hindering your ability to fish and properly evaluate how the jig is behaving underwater. Large bobbers also make proper mending near impossible due to their increased drag in fast water.

The best bobber I've found for fishing the 1/32- 1/16 ounce jig is

The 1/16-ounce Stuart Steelhead Bullet works great in low, clear water, and fishes well below a West Coast Float strike indicator.

the strike indicator bobber crafted by West Coast Floats. This small bobber reacts well on the water and is easy to see.

When casting upstream, you want to get your bobber floating vertically as quick as possible. Initially, when working a hole, watch your bobber closely. If the top tips downstream, your jig is hitting the bottom. As the jig hits bottom, the current forces the bobber ahead of the jig and drag forces it to capsize. Such action makes enticing a bite very difficult.

If your bobber tips upstream, mend the line. A bobber tips upstream when too much line lies on the water's surface, creating drag. If this happens, mend the line by lifting the rod and rolling it toward the bobber to eat up the slack. This is where the 12-foot noodle rod comes in handy, as it allows you to aggressively move more line, thereby working more water.

One long section of river routinely found me anchoring at three key points to drift fish the entire stretch. With bobber and jigs I can now anchor in the middle, cast far upstream, and let it drift way downstream. In all, I can cover over 100 yards of prime water without moving an inch, and it can be done by boat or from the bank.

I can't stress enough the degree of advantage afforded to the angler who invests in a long rod and good spinning reel. If you don't already have one, get a quality open-face reel with a good drag that will hold a couple hundred yards of line. A reel of this magnitude will allow you to cover more water and hang on to those fish once hooked.

Fighting a summer steelhead on a jig is like nothing I've experienced in terms of power and aggression. These fish hit with such vigor they set the hook themselves, which is what allows you to catch them 100 yards downstream. Whether steelhead think a jig is prey or enemy, they assault to kill. Multiple leaps on each hookup are the rule rather than the exception, thus making a smooth and reliable drag system a must.

Upwards of 90% of jig and bobber fishing is looselined. That is, the bail is flipped open and the line free to spool off. This ensures there is no drag on the line, allowing your bobber to ride vertically, holding the jig in a natural position as it drifts downstream. From the top of the cast, to the bottom of the drift, I rarely reel. The only times I reel are to take up slack, set the hook, or to reel in at the end of a drift. Because the spool is opened when fishing, it's imperative to watch the bobber closely, for once it disappears, quickly closing the reel and taking up the slack is crucial to hooking the fish.

The ideal mainline is one that rides high in the water. Floating line lets you mend and fish more water, whereas monofilaments sink and create too much drag, thus impeding the action of the jig. I prefer Berkley's 20-pound Fireline, and have found this to be the premier way to go when jig fishing. This line is excellent for holding the bobber stop in place and is extremely buoyant; often the entire line remains atop the surface. The longer you can keep your line floating, the easier it is to mend, thus, the more water you fish. Flame green is the color of choice, optimizing visibility.

Leaders are a different story and can be ever-changing with water conditions, but I've been pleased with P-Line's fluorocarbon selection when it comes to clearwater situations. This tough, highly abrasion-resistant material has low stretch and great sensitivity, possesses a fast sink rate and performs extremely well in all situations. Early in the year, when the water is high and the fish full of life, a 10-pound leader is ideal. I know of anglers who'll go up to 12 pound in extreme conditions. As summer progresses, low, clear water can make fishing jigs a challenge; drop to eight-pound fluorocarbon leader. In very low, crystal-clear water, four-pound copolymer leader can be the way to go. With a 12-foot noodler, the rod absorbs much of the fight, allowing for the use of such a light leader.

Anglers should note, due to the lack of line stretch, a reel with a reliable drag system is recommended. If, in using this setup you find fish are breaking off, reevaluate your equipment and the amount of pressure you're putting on them. With a good rod and reel combination, there's no reason to be breaking off fish.

There are several jigs on the market, but the only one I use–along with many converted jig fanatics–is the Stuart Steelhead Bullet, personally crafted by Bret Stuart. Bret hand-ties each jig, gets a nice tight wrap and uses only the best, most reactive marabou and matching head paints. By utilizing only the sharp,

Collared jigs in the 1/32- to 1/4-ounce range allow plastic worms from two to six inches in length to be fished.

wispy portions of marabou, a most attractive jig is created. Stuart ties his jigs so only 1/4 of an inch of marabou hangs past the hook, greatly increasing the strike-to-hook ratio. The result is a quality jig that steelhead can't resist.

Stuart has also developed a jig for fishing plastic worms. Instead of tying a marabou body on the jig, Stuart wraps a long-hackled collar just below the head of the jig. Equipped with a bait keeper, the hook itself snugly holds a plastic worm in place cast after cast. These worm collar jigs are fished just like traditional jigs, and the range of sight afforded by the addition of a bright pink or orange worm makes them deadly in high or off-color waters. Worms fished on these jigs range in size from two to six inches, with the three- and four-inch worms being a favorite among many.

Prior to fishing with any jig, try offsetting the hook—turning the barb to one side or the other—so it's not in direct alignment with the jig head. This will result in a higher percentage of hookups.

Jig fishing is a style that allows you to work vast expanses of water. I've fished along, above, and below jig fishermen. Keep in mind, when jig fishing popular spots, other anglers have every right to work the same area. It's easy to longline in front of other anglers, but avoid it. Be courteous, fish what water you can without infringing on others, and everyone will have an enjoyable time on the water. If you find yourself with the urge to fish large segments of water, move to where there are fewer people.

The author with a limit of steelhead taken on a Stuart Steelhead Bullet. These fish were caught from the same hole in less than an hour.

Jig and bobber fishing turned over a new leaf in my steelhead fishing life and is one of my favorite ways to catch these awesome fish. It's a tool every angler should have in their repertoire. It's also one of the easiest techniques to learn. When equipping yourself for jig and bobber fishing, closely adhere to the gear specifications presented here. It won't cost much more to do it right, and will lead to less frustration and more success. Once you get the hang of jig fishing, you'll be glad you took the time to set yourself up properly.

Chapter 7
Tossing Hardware

If you enjoy covering vast stretches of water and constantly being on the move, tossing lures is for you. It's the simplest approach to steelhead fishing there is, requiring only swivels and lures to be toted around. For bank anglers, having the freedom to roam and thoroughly explore a river is optimized when fishing with lures, as little downtime impedes your movement.

In addition to covering lots of water over a short time period, there are other benefits to casting lures for steelhead. Spinners, especially, result in very few hang ups, as they are worked near the bottom, but not on the bottom. Lures also trigger bites from a great distance. The flashy presentation elicits a response unlike any bait.

One summer day, Dad and I spotted several steelhead holding on the upper end of a tailout. We rolled eggs by them, parked sand shrimp off their noses, and nothing; not even a glance. Dad switched to a blue wobbler and as soon as it hit the water a fish was making a wake for it. I wasted no time tying on a green wobbler, and was met with the same result. Within a dozen casts we boated four fish, but the impressive thing was not the limit, rather how far each fish traveled to attack the lures. Of the four fish, every one traveled no less than three feet to nail the lure. Mind you, these were the same fish that, moments earlier, were having the best baits known to steelhead passed inches from their snouts without so much as a look. This is just one example of how effective lures can be.

The Benefits

Lures are ideal for searching for fish, something that's tough for bait anglers to accomplish at a comparable rate. By this I mean, not only does the lure tosser cover a great deal of real estate by walking, but on each successive cast as well. Lures can be thrown great distances, and unlike drift fishing, you don't have to cover the same water twice.

Because lures pull fish from a wide range, the distance between consecutive casts can be greater. When dissecting a river by drifting eggs, the distance separating casts is measured in inches. When working water with hardware, the gap between casts is measured in feet. This statistic alone shows how considerably more water can be covered by fishing lures. Couple this with the fact that an incredibly high percentage of steelhead hit lures on their first pass, and you can get a feel for how much water can be covered in a day. This is why lures are so effective when seeking fish that may be spread throughout a river.

Lures also allow water to be fished that can't otherwise be probed by other means. Log-jammed sections, those areas with large boulders directly in the path of the current and deep, dead sections of water, are all ideal for working lures. These are waters that are tough to steer plugs into and make drift fishing a nightmare for hangups.

Rooster Tails are a favorite among summer steelheaders, and with good reason.

Working Lures

Addressing specific styles, makes and brands of lures is a book in itself; something best left to authors who have penned volumes on such topics. A general rule applied by many lure anglers refers to presenting the largest possible selection without spooking fish. Doing so not only allows you to cover more water, it pulls fish from greater distances by honing in on their visual and auditory senses. Throwing heavier hardware also allows longer casts to be made, thus more water is blanketed. But there are others who feel using smaller, less disturbing lures is the way to go. I let the river be my guide. In clear, shallow sections, smaller spinners are effective; in deep, fast waters, big spoons are preferred.

If you believe, or can see that fish are in an area but not reacting to your offering, try changing colors and/or sizes of your presentation. If that silver #4, copper-bladed Metric doesn't produce, try a different color, perhaps a size or two smaller. At the same time, if fishing clear, low water, or water receiving direct sunlight and forcing fish into shallower, scattered water, drop to a less intrusive lure size.

Where spinners are casted and retrieved in a manner allowing for optimal water coverage with minimal hangup, spoons are presented in a different fashion. The urge to fish spoons like spinners can be tough to thwart, but will be rewarded with success when done properly.

A spoon is designed with the intention of cutting through water in erratic, non-rhythmical action, unlike that of a spinner. As such, spoons should be fished differently. Applying as little line tension as possible is ideal when casting spoons; negating the old fishing adage, "keep a tight line." The tighter the line on a spoon, the less active the spoon will fish. By allowing a spoon to move freely as much as possible throughout the duration of a cast, the fluttering action that results will be maximized. You should barely be able to feel that a spoon is on the other end of your line, except when reeling or lifting the lure over structure, or off the bottom. Don't be afraid to reel, lift, and let the spoon drop. The unsteady motion of the falling lure, enhanced by the ever-changing underwater currents, is what entices fish to strike.

While baitcasting reels are optimal for most steelhead fishing, spinning reels are ideal for casting lures. As short, pinpoint casting accuracy with lightweight lures is often required, this can most efficiently be achieved by using an open-faced reel with a high retrieve ratio.

Casting lures is a great way to cover vast amounts of river in search of fish.

The best, overall advice for any lure angler is to keep casting and moving. My father and his college fishing buddy would stick a handful of lures in their pockets, place their fishing licenses in plastic baggies beneath their baseball caps, and swim to where they wished to fish. This approach, though extreme and not recommended for everyone, got them into steelhead on a regular basis, and kept them refreshed on those 100°, hot summer days.

Only by constantly being on the prowl, hitting any and every possible bit of water capable of holding fish, will the objective of lure fishing be fully realized.

Chapter 8
Dragging Flies

More than any other element of summer steelhead fishing, pursuing them with fly gear receives the most ink. There are volumes written on patterns and tactical approaches, so we're not going to delve into those aspects here. But there is a technique worth noting, one that works well in fast waters.

Dragging—technically, backtrolling—flies is nothing new to steelheading, but it is an approach that is definitely underused. If you own a boat, the rest is simple. The major benefit of dragging flies is that it allows you to fish water otherwise inaccessible to plugging and drifting techniques. Those shallow riffles holding fish on sunny days may be tough working a plug in, and positioning to drift it may spook fish; gently backing a fly into such settings may be your best bet.

Dragging flies in classic steelhead water—tailouts, breaks, flats, even deeper, clear sections of river—is also effective. Plugging water in the three- to ten-foot depth range is ideal for working flies. But where backing flies downstream pays dividends, is when fishing water you might otherwise deem unfishable and pass right by.

A Muddler pattern coupled with a bead-head fly is an effective summer steelhead combination.

There's a particular straight stretch of river I like to fish that receives very little pressure. Nearly all the boats push down river to the next riffle. But what they don't see is a three-foot deep, transparent stretch of water with slight surface chop, teaming with fish. For a 200-yard stretch, numerous little flats exist within the riffle, and granted, while spotting the fish is tough, they are always there. This is too shallow to work a plug in, but backing flies down to the metalheads is lethal.

The Technique

Unlike the pinpoint accuracy necessary when maneuvering plugs into position, backtrolling flies is a bit more forgiving. Working the boat at a speed about one-third that of water flow is ideal, though this may vary within certain sections of the river. Due to the amount of drag placed on and dispersed throughout the fly line, keeping the flies working in alignment as they move downstream is not as taxing when compared to pulling plugs.

However, as in plugging, dragging flies requires that you look ahead, assessing the water, predicting where fish will be holding, placing the patterns in the exact target spot. It's easy to get lazy with this techniques, as there are few hangups and less effort is required to skipper the craft, but don't let it happen. Concentrating on the task at hand and always thinking ahead—where you want the flies, at what speed you wish to present them and where fish will likely be—is critical to making this approach successful.

Dragging, or backtrolling, flies is gaining popularity among summer steelheaders.

Depending on water clarity, stripping 20 to 30 feet of dry fly line is optimal. In shallow stretches, you may wish to extend the distance to 35 or even 40 feet, for fear the fish may see the boat and spook. Whatever distance you decide on, run both rods the same distance. If there are two passengers in the front of the boat, three rods can be run—one out each side, one over the bow—but in turbulent waters, keeping them separated can be a challenge.

Because shallower, clear sections of water are worked when dragging flies, the skipper must finesse the boat downstream. Quiet entry and exiting of the oars is important, as the objective is to sneak up on the fish without being detected. In tumultuous riffles, such as those in which you'd pull plugs, boat noise is typically masked by the sounds of the river. But as you transition into calmer waters, don't forget to go easy on the oars, you don't want any unforced errors.

The Gear

A 5- to 7-weight fly rod and a matching floating line is all you need to get started for dragging flies. Utilizing a floating line is critical for achieving proper depth which ultimately places the fly in the all-important Snell's Window. This window is the 97° angle mentioned in Chapter 6, and is the angle of vision a fish sees from underwater. As light touches the surface, the 180° angle receiving the light compresses it into a 97° window. The angle of the viewing window is constant, regardless of depth. Thus, a fish holding on the bottom of an eight-foot hole will have double the sight window of one holding at four feet. Floating lines allow the water to be evenly depressed, presenting the flies on a plane, something more likely to be noticed by fish. Steelhead also have the ability to see directly in front of them, picking up food and impediments as they approach from upstream. Knowing this, weighted flies and sinking-tip lines can prove valuable in appropriate waters.

Nine-foot 4X, 3X or 2X tippets are good choices, and which one you use will be determined by the river and the tenacity of the fish. When fishing a river with big wild fish, I know they'll fight harder than hatchery stock, taking me all over, so I will go with heavier tippet. If I'm on a river with few obstructions and a nice graveled bottom, a lighter weight tippet can be employed.

Steelhead can be taken on a variety of patterns.
The author relied on a flashy streamer for this fish.

Pulling a double-fly setup is very effective, where the top pattern serves as an attractor. Two to five feet should separate the two flies, with the attractor being tied to a six- to eight-inch leader. Matching the patterns to respective aquatic life in the river being fished is a good idea. In most of the rivers I fish, using a silver tinsel bodied sculpin or muddler pattern on a size 10 hook seems to be the ticket for a great attractor; in fact, these patterns take the majority of hits. Dropping a couple sizes, the trailing fly can be any pattern you have confidence in, that would be used for big trout, or one you know correlates to food found in the system. Bead-head patterns such as Copper Johns are popular, all-around choices.

Another pattern that can be successfully presented on this fly setup is a 1/32-ounce Stuart Steelhead Bullet. This lightweight jig acts as weighted flies and when fished alone, can really capture the attention of steelhead. The bright patterns in which these jigs are tied often seem to produce bites when nothing else will.

Often overlooked as a fly fishing alternative, dragging flies is something every steelhead angler should have in their repertoire. Once you acquire the gear, the rest is simple to learn, which is what makes this effective style of fishing so enjoyable.

The 1/32-ounce Stuart Steelhead Bullet is finding a home in the vests of many devoted fly anglers. This fish came from Deep Creek, on Alaska's Kenai Peninsula.

Catching a summer steelhead on a fly is something every serious angler must experience. The author took this fish on California's Klamath River.

Chapter 9
The Driftboat Bonus

If you're serious about becoming the best, well-rounded steelheader possible, a driftboat is an essential tool. If you already own one, using it to its fullest potential is the objective. There are several aspects to consider when buying and operating a driftboat, and we'll elaborate on some of those points in this chapter.

First and foremost, a river boat is not to be looked upon as an easy-to-operate vessel, though it can be. Rivers are powerful forces of nature, and there's more to manning a river boat than simply floating it downstream, happily bouncing through rapids. Every year anglers fall victim to river boat tragedies, even veterans pushing their luck have lost their lives.

Safety is the most important element to consider when buying and running a driftboat. If you're apprehensive about buying a boat, maybe now isn't the time. But if you're fired-up and ready to go, there's no better time than right now to purchase that boat and peer into the many windows of fortune that present themselves through driftboat fishing.

The rewards of fishing from a driftboat are numerous,
not the least of which is the solitude it can provide.

Taking the Plunge

Purchasing a driftboat is a big move. Before doing so, spend some time on the river with an experienced oarsman. This will provide enough familiarity for you to properly evaluate the worth of a boat, in terms of how to maneuver the craft, what fishing benefits it has to offer, and whether or not you feel compelled to buy such an item. This valuable experience will also make you sound like a pro when trying to convince your wife the investment is a must.

Determining what style and brand of boat to get boils down to personal preference. Wood, fiberglass and metals are all materials from which driftboats are built. Having been born and raised on Oregon's McKenzie River, home to the wooden driftboat, I'm somewhat partial to wooden boats. The light weight of a wooden boat makes for fast reaction time on the water, and is easier for the oarsman to handle in all types of situations. But the upkeep demanded, and the fact it can't take the punishment delivered on other boats, can be a drawback.

Determine what rivers you intend to use a driftboat on. If you're looking at sticking with a few calm streams, and have the time to care for a wooden boat and a place to store it during the winter, this may be the type of craft you're looking for. But if you intend on hitting as many rivers in as many regions of the country as you can, at various times of the year, a metal or fiberglass boat may be the way to go.

The only major drawbacks of metal boats are their excessive weight and noisy nature. But the decreased upkeep and durability make them a gem. If you fish alone, fiberglass—being lighter than metal boats yet demanding less upkeep than wood—may be what you're looking for.

Ask other boat owners their preference and why. Seek out advice from experienced boaters to help determine what type of boat is best for you. Inquiring at boating shops, through ads placed in fishing magazines, and classified ads are good starting points. Check the sales section of newspapers, often times great buys can be had on all kinds of boats. You can spend anywhere from $500 to $6,000 for a boat/trailer combination, depending on if it's used or brand new with all the bells and whistles. You may also opt to go the customized route, which gets even more spendy, but if you're looking to keep this boat for several years, such a decision may be worth considering.

Once you've determined the type of boat to get, oars are your next purchase. If they come with the boat, great; if not, there's some research to be done. Whatever oars you decide on, get three of them. Never launch a boat without an extra oar onboard. I once watched a boat pick its way down Oregon's Rogue River. Finagling his way through a boulder patch, the oarsman had an oar pop out of the lock and yanked from his hand. He had plenty of time to grab another oar, but with no extra onboard, could only pray. Unfortunately, the boat capsized in what turned out to be a life-threatening situation for the three people onboard. No matter what the cost, get that third oar. An extra oar lock is also wise; if one breaks you'll have a spare.

Remember, an oar is nothing more than a simple machine, a lever, that allows you to move the object upon which it pivots. Therefore, the longer the oar, the less effort the oarsman exerts, the more efficient the work output. A set of nine- to ten-foot oars, be they wood, aluminum, graphite or fiberglass are optimal.

A setup to prevent the oar lock from slipping out is recommended, especially on fast moving steelhead rivers.

Ultimately, the length of oar you choose is determined by boat size and style, as well as by the types of rivers you plan on fishing. A 17 foot, wide-bottomed guide model boat will take longer oars than a 14 foot, narrow boat.

Wooden oars are great, look sharp, and hold-up well if taken care of. But if they break, they are tough to mend. Many aluminum and graphite oars though, have paddles that can be replaced should damage occur. Whatever oars you select, invest in a pair of oar locks with a locking system, to prevent them from popping out in rough water. A rubber collar slid on the oars will also keep them from slipping through the oar locks, keeping the oars hanging straight in the water when anchored, helping to stabilize the boat.

As for anchor systems, there are many ways to go. If there's a chance you'll run a motor off the back, be certain the anchor is offset to allow room for motor mounting. The only drawback with this arrangement is it requires a side or back-pull rope system. Side pulling rope systems—the most commonly used setup—are fine, but they do place strain on one's back and can be tough to retrieve in fast water, where getting your hands on the oars as quickly as possible is necessary.

My favorite anchor system is one that runs directly out the back of the boat and is mounted between the legs, at the feet, of the oarsman. This allows for a direct pull, where legs and arms do the work on the 20- to 30-pound mass,

*Both anchor systems allow the oarsman to use his body while facing straight ahead.
These are preferred over setups that put the strain on one arm and twist the torso;
they are also faster reacting, a factor to consider when fishing heavy rapids.*

not your back. No torso twisting is required, and the time from when the anchor is lifted to when control of the oars are taken is minimal, a definite bonus when it comes to working fast water.

Carry no less than 75 feet of anchor rope onboard, and do not tie a knot in the free end. Should an anchor get hung in turbulent waters, where retrieving it is not an option, you can gain control of the oars and let the anchor line slip through the pulleys, out of the boat. If the anchor does get hung to the point you're taking risky chances by trying to work it free, cut the line. A few dollars worth of lead is not worth losing your entire boat. I lost a friend to this scenario, and he was a seasoned boater who knew better.

The Benefits & SOP

A driftboat allows you to access waters that are inaccessible to bank anglers, either because of bank structure or private lands. A wider array of techniques can be applied when fishing from a boat, a proven fact that aids in increasing your catch. Pulling plugs, backbouncing, backtrolling baits and flies, and even diversified drift fishing techniques can all be better applied from a boat than from shore. I've even found the hook-to-land ratio on fish to dramatically increase from a boat. The position of a boat relative to the hole being fished, and the elevated angle at which the rod is worked from a boat, compound to result in a high percentage of hooked and landed steelhead.

But the most critical element for success when fishing from a driftboat lies in the hands of the oarsman. The skipper must be smooth, quiet, and know what to search for when positioning a boat for fishing. Such aspects of the

Driftboats can take you to bank-fishing sites anglers can't reach on foot.

sport can only be acquired through spending time on the water, learning from others, and manning a boat yourself.

While in calm waters, practice learning what a boat is capable of doing, familiarizing yourself with its limitations. Knowing how a boat reacts to every move of your oars is crucial in developing a rowing style that allows you to determine what the boat can really do. The ultimate goal is to be able to row the boat without thinking about it. With practice, instinctual rowing skills will develop and will make the river a safer place. In some fast water rivers, you don't always have time to think about what the next stroke of the oar should be; rather, the next move is a reaction. When you reach this stage, you'll know it. Not only will you feel safer and more confident in the boat, you'll catch more fish.

Proper weight distribution of gear and passengers in the boat is important for the oarsman to be aware of. You don't want the bow or stern too heavy, as this causes drag, hampering control. At the same time, your side-to-side balance should be even. Passengers must be sitting in their chairs, legs forward, facing straight ahead, especially when rough waters are in view.

By maintaining a state of equilibrium within the vessel, total control can be declared by the skipper. The more control the skipper has, the safer the ride for all involved.

In terms of the standard operating procedure when it comes to drift-boats, always keep the boat in position so the bow and stern are pulled away from danger. Only on rare occasions should you push the bow of a boat out of a dangerous situation. The key is maximizing your reaction time, and this is done by pulling the boat against the current, not pushing with it while being carried downstream. No matter what, when amid a boulder patch, working through shelves or picking your way through brushy banked areas—keep the boat positioned in such a way that you can pull away from obstacles in a nanosecond's notice.

Wherever you drift, be certain to abide by all boating laws, for the safety of all onboard. Life jackets, a whistle, and other state required gear is a must. A second anchor, garbage bags for removal of fish entrails and 100 feet of extra rope, are also great ideas, as is a throw cushion or other floatation devices. The extra rope comes in handy when pulling your boat out of unimproved ramps, helping someone free a hung anchor, or rescuing other anglers who run into some bad luck. The extra anchor is nice when on rivers whose currents are such that a boat is more firmly held in place by a duo setup.

Through time and practice, you'll learn how to hit the heads of riffles, distinguish between fishable and unfishable waters, maneuver through log-jammed obstacle courses and more. When it comes to riffles, take extra care not to progress too far into a riffle prior to fishing it. Oftentimes steelhead nose into the head of a riffle, and these fish are often passed over by boaters. Going by such fish not only spooks them, it puts you past the point where they can't be fished anyway.

While plugging, working divers and various other tactics are specifically addressed in this book, don't overlook the options of boondogging and side-drifting from a boat. Early in the season—or when dams have opened their spillways—boondogging can be effective in long, slower moving stretches of water often found between classic, fast moving steelhead waters. This is where boondogging is most effective.

Situate the boat off to the side of the target area where fish are anticipated to be. Let the boat drift at the rate at which the river is flowing. This is a fast presentation. All anglers in the boat, starting with the person closest to the targeted fish site, cast their drift fishing gear at a 45° angle upstream, letting the line come in contact with the bottom. Once the bottom is felt, take up the slack, letting the terminal gear move downstream with the boat. The terminal gear will only occasionally come in contact with the bottom, but it's always in the steelhead's line of sight, which is what makes this approach so effective.

Side-drifting is similar to boondogging, but requires the skipper to row the boat, not fish. In doing so, the boat is held at about half the speed of water flow. This leaves the passenger(s) to basically drift fish as the boat moves downstream. By using considerably less lead than what you'd use if anchored and drift fishing the same stretch, a natural presentation just off the bottom can be had.

Side-drifting also varies from boondogging in that casts are typically delivered straight out or downstream from the boat. Due to the lighter terminal gear used in side-drifting, a completed drift will be had, meaning successive casts are required. This is a great method when moving through large sections of clear water.

When used and respected as a tool of the sport, a driftboat presents thrills and excitement like no other form of steelhead fishing. Fishing from a driftboat takes you into the peace and solitude so many anglers yearn for. Distancing yourself from crowds, hearing the lap of riffles tickle the boat; there's simply nothing like being on the river, taking in nature's wonders.

An often-overlooked site by driftboaters is where a slick leads into a riffle.
Plugging the head of a riffle, prior to dropping over it, can yield fish,
as they often nose-up against the rocks and hold in the rippling water.

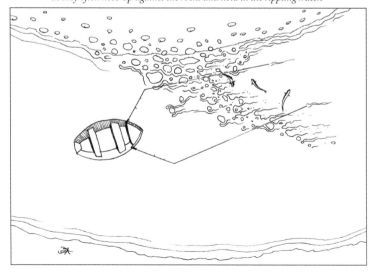

Chapter 10
Pulling Plugs

Two theories apply to plug fishing: It's great for beginning anglers and it's great for veterans. Though at extreme ends of the spectrum, both theories are correct. The beauty of plug fishing is that it allows any and all anglers the opportunity to catch fish.

For beginning oarsmen and passengers, pulling plugs is a good way to learn steelhead waters. Figuring out where fish lay and move are critical elements to becoming a more complete student of the sport, and plug fishing helps teach this. By experimenting with boat maneuvering, fishing diverse types of water amid varied river levels, and systematically plotting plug coloration to fit water conditions, novice anglers become educated on much more than just pulling plugs.

At the same time, many seasoned anglers who have plug fishing down to a science believe this method is the best way to consistently catch fish. Let's look at the key elements that go into becoming a serious summer steelhead plug angler.

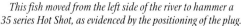

*This fish moved from the left side of the river to hammer a
35 series Hot Shot, as evidenced by the positioning of the plug.*

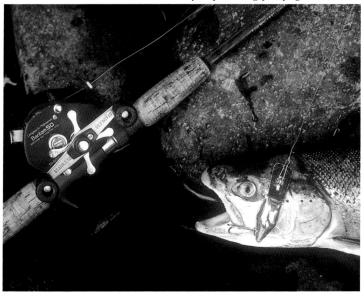

The Plugs

While plugs can be cast and retrieved from the bank, or run off a sideplaner from the bank, this chapter will focus on operating plugs from a boat. With several varieties of plugs on the market, most anglers have their choices narrowed down to a half-dozen or so. By far, the most popular plug used on these fish is the Hot Shot. Available in various sizes, those found in the tackle boxes of many summer steelheaders include the 30, 35 and 40 series. With it's built-in rattle, the 35 series and 1/4-ounce Hot Shots are a favorite when irritating a fish is the objective. A 25 series plug is also popular in big, heavy water. The 30 series Hot Shot is perhaps the most versatile, being used in all waters except for select deep holes and a few clear, shallow riffles. The 40 series Hot Shots are as small as most anglers will go for steelhead. But don't overlook the size 50 Hot Shots, they are ideal in very low, clear waters.

When levels drop and the water becomes clear, a small-profiled plug like this 50 series Hot Shot can be dynamite.

Wiggle Warts and Wee Warts are also good to have onboard. Wiggle Warts work in deep, fast moving water, while the smaller Wee Warts produce well in shallow river situations. Tadpollies and Hot-N-Tots are good plug choices and offer varied action in medium to fast water.

In slower moving waters, Kwikfish and Flatfish may be the ticket. Kwikfish in sizes K10 and K12, with the K12 being the deeper diving of the two, are good choices. Flatfish of the X5 and larger U20 sizes are also good bets. Deep holes where current flow is minimal, killing the action of most other plugs, is where the Kwikfish and Flatfish earn their money.

A wide plug selection–in style, size, and color, will help prepare you for just about any type of water conditions.

As for which colors work best, there are several theories. Some anglers carry at least one plug of every color crammed into their tackle box. Others use only three or four they know will catch fish.

On cloudy days, gold- and copper-colored plugs are good choices, while sunny days should see silver plugs putting in the most time. In shallow, clear waters, natural colored plugs like crawfish or trout imitations can be deadly. In deeper, clear waters, blue and green plugs are good choices. Pirate-colored plugs are very effective, and are versatile under several conditions.

People often ask what my favorite summer steelheading plug is. Every angler asked this question may have a different response. Whether it's the color or the unique action of that particular plug that catches fish is a point of debate. But if I were stuck on the river with only one plug to fish, it would be silver with a red head. Taking a permanent marker, color the bill of a silver Hot Shot red. A 30, 35 or 40 series Hot Shot with a red bill is one I'll always try having in the water, especially if there are one or two passengers in the boat.

Since I use this color combination so much, does it mean the silver bodied, red-billed plug is the best steelheading plug? Yes, and no. Who is to say, had I been running a white Wee Wart, or different colored Hot Shot that I wouldn't pick up the same fish. One will never know the answer to this question. The bottom line when it comes to plug selection is: Use what you have the most confidence in.

Some anglers meticulously use an airbrush to put their own designs on plugs, using only those patterns. Others may paint the bill black to give contrast to the lighter colored body. Pink plugs, no matter what the style, are favored by several anglers. Many plug fanatics even have a preferred design and color for various rivers. Don't be afraid to experiment around and find what works for you. Once you've discovered that magic plug, use it with conviction.

The Setup

Prior to fishing, most plugs fresh from the package need alterations. The majority of plugs on the market are designed for bass fishing. Stripping down plugs—either removing both sets of hooks or one of them—and equipping them for steelhead is important.

Dropping the hook back, to barb those short strikes, is perhaps the most important alteration to be made on a plug. With the use of 'O' rings, bead chain swivels, and barrel swivels, hooks can be attached that trail well behind the tail of each plug. A single Siwash hook is preferred by many anglers. When struck by a fish, the Siwash goes flat in their mouth, allowing for a penetrating hook set. With treble hooks, fish can work the points against one another, resulting in a loss. Trebles can also be less forgiving when bringing a flailing fish into the net.

O-rings, oval rings, split rings and bead chains are good devices to drop the hooks back on plugs, into a more effective strike zone.

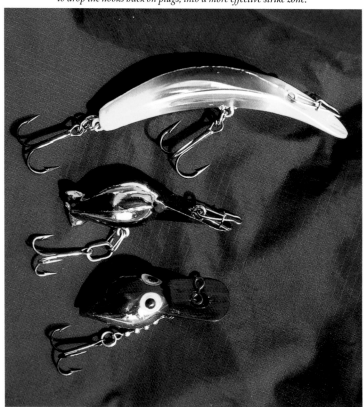

Sometimes, on plugs like Hot Shots, treble hooks may be the only option due to a loss of tuning that's created when they are removed. Whatever hook you do switch to, be certain it is as sharp as possible. Always have a file on hand and hone those hooks whenever necessary. Before fishing any plug, make certain it's tuned. Feed a few feet of line out, pulling it against the current to make sure it's running straight. If not, adjust the eye of the plug accordingly. To whichever side the plug is pulling, slightly rotate the eye in the opposite direction until the plug runs true. Tuning instructions come on the boxes of most plugs.

When tying to the leader or mainline, I go directly to the eye of the plug or into the round eye snap. If attaching to the eye, use a loop knot to optimize the plug's action. If tying to the round snap, like on a Hot Shot, an improved clinch knot is a good choice. Don't attach a snap swivel to the plug as it inhibits the natural action.

Plugs can be tied directly to the mainline or to a leader. If going with a leader, affix a size 7 barrel swivel to the end of the mainline, followed by five to eight feet of leader. The barrel swivel guards against line twist when a fish is hooked and offers the luxury of dropping to lighter pound test leader if desired.

Specially crafted plugging rods are made, though are not necessary. I know of guides who still use 30-year-old fiberglass rods for plugging due to their animated movement when fished. On the other hand, I like the backbone in plugging rods. I look for a rod that sets the hook itself, and that is rigid enough to lead a fish into the net in fast water. Whatever route you go, keep in mind a light-action tip is prime for interpreting plug behavior. As for line, I prefer 10-12 pound high visibility monofilament when plugging, with an 8-10 pound leader. Using a high visibility line is good for the oarsman, as it allows him to better observe the plugs and how they are reacting. Dropping to a lighter weight mainline, say from 12 to 10 pound, will also allow the plug to run deeper, as the smaller diameter line creates less drag. If you know fish are around and you're not hitting them with 12- or 15-pound mainline, try dropping to a smaller diameter line, it will allow you to get down.

If running two plugs, positioning the rods next to, or slightly behind the passenger seat, is a preferred location. Not only does this give the oarsman a better view of the action, it puts the rods in easy reach should he need to quickly react to a situation. If the rods can't be slipped between the gunnels, rod holders are a must. Though it's exciting to hold a rod when plugging, it makes it tough for the oarsman to read how the plug is working, thus anticipating what his next move should be. If you insist on holding a rod, lay the butt section across your lap, with the rod steadied on the gunnels.

If three people are in the boat, a third rod can be placed in a rod holder atop the fly deck, or on the floor, between the oarsman and the passengers. Many oarsman like having the rod butt near their feet so they can grab it when the hit comes.

One of the most common errors in plug fishing occurs when anglers let out too much line. The more line that is out, the higher the plug rides in the water and the less effective its action. The maximum distance I'll let out a plug is 60 feet, and this is primarily in clear, shallow water. Thirty to 45 feet are my preferred distances. At these lengths the plugs really dig in, working far enough ahead to illicit a strike before the boat has a chance to spook a fish.

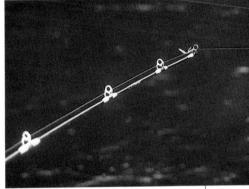

Prior to hitting the river, make sure you know your plugging distances for each rod. The simplest approach is to string the desired length of line from your spool, say 45 feet. Measure the distance and tie a bobber stop at this point, just past the top guide of your rod. When letting out line to fish there's no need to count the number of passes on the reel or to guess your distance, for as soon as the thread passes the last guide, stop.

Tying a bobber stop at the precise distance you wish to fish will ensure uniformity when plugging; this is especially effective when running two or more rods.

Counting the number of times your line passes back and forth across the baitcasting spool is the most common method of determining your plugging distance. The drawback with this method comes when you real a plug toward the boat to clean it, and the debris drops off after riding a short distance on the surface. Now, rather than dropping the plug back down to continue fishing, you must bring it in, letting it back out, counting off the proper distance.

Whether you fish two or three plugs, running them all at the same distance is vital. This allows the oarsman to know exactly where the plugs are at all times. In narrow boats, running the middle, third plug, a foot or two farther will prevent tangles from occurring when the boat's position changes.

Fishing Plugs

With the rods, plugs and boat properly equipped, you're ready to fish. Plug fishing is something that must be loved by the skipper, for he's the one pumping on the oars. A full day of plug fishing takes its toll on the body, especially on blistering summer days.

It's the oarsman who is responsible for nearly all the fishing when pulling plugs. The role of the passenger is threefold: To make sure the plugs are properly working, to keep an eye out for obstacles in the river, and to look for any sign of fish. Funny thing is, the oarsman usually detects these things before the passenger, for he's the one most dialed in.

If plugging a river from side-to-side, the speed of the boat should be kept slightly less than that of the speed of the water being fished. Excessive pressure sends the plugs too deep. Lack of pressure keeps them suspended too high. A steady vibration of the rod tip is the goal, striving to maintain that rhythm the entire time. If plugging straight downstream, trolling about 1/3 the speed of the current is a good, general speed for summer runs.

Proper placement of rod holders is important when plugging. They should be set where the oarsman can clearly see the rod tips, yet where passengers can quickly grab the poles.

The most critical error made while plugging—I occasionally catch myself doing it—is cutting angles too sharp when working the water. When maneuvering the boat from one side of the river to the other, across the current, the angle should be slight. If there's any bend in the line, the angle is too steep. You should never have to sit and wait for your line to catch up to the boat. Watch boaters who routinely catch fish, they move slowly across a stream, keeping that line tight. This is also true when plugging from a sled.

In a driftboat, the back end of the boat always points where you want to go. This angle should be kept very slight. When working across, and downstream, maintaining the proper speed and angle are vital. The oarsman should put the plugs in the precise spot of where a steelhead may lie, and this can only be done by accurately positioning the boat every moment those plugs are in the river.

The idea is to trigger an aggressive, reactive bite, or push steelhead to the bottom of the plugging hole. When driven downstream to the point they won't drop any further, steelhead will often attack a plug out of frustration. It's the job of the oarsman to not let the fish slip by, though this is inevitable much of the time. This is why it's imperative the oarsman dissects a body of water and tediously work it over.

In plugging, covering as much water as possible is the objective, and this is best done with two boats. If a pair of boats can work straight downstream, side-by-side, backtrolling a wall of a half-dozen plugs dramatically increases the odds of catching fish. This technique not only cuts down on the number of escape routes a steelhead may use, but when it does bump fish, they often run smack into a neighboring plug, which they often strike out of aggression.

Working two driftboats side-by-side allows anglers to present
a wall of plugs. If this approach doesn't draw an initial strike,
it often forces fish downstream, whereupon they attack out of rage.

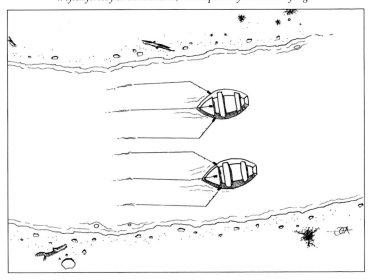

Tailouts, slicks, seams between fast and slow water, boulder patches, heads of holes, cut banks, shadowed edges, ledges, shallow and deep riffles are all ideal plugging waters. Deep holes, eddies, boiling waters and boiling sections bordering fast water, along with fast water where it's difficult to hold a boat, are not good plugging choices.

By paying close attention to river details, situating the boat precisely where you want it, and by taking a systematic approach to plug fishing, your level of proficiency can rapidly increase. The more you learn about plug fishing through trial and error, the more fish you'll hook.

Kwikfish and Flatfish should not be overlooked when plugging for steelhead; the author has found them to be particularly effective in high off-color waters.

Chapter 11
Diver-and-Bait Setups

*U*nder certain circumstances, working a diver and bait for summer steelhead can be highly effective. They are especially efficient in waters that are deep and fast moving. Drift fishing in such areas can shred bait in just a few casts; gently slipping a diver and bait into the same waters can keep a bait fishing for an extended period of time, ultimately increasing the chance of a strike.

Murky waters and deep flowing holes are ideal places to run a diver and bait. At the same time, very clear waters are good for backing a diver into as the presentation is discrete, meaning the chances of spooking fish diminishes. Classic, fast-rolling plugging water and tailouts can also be good diver and bait locales; places I've pulled many steelhead from over the years.

While the presentation of a diver and bait from a boat is similar to pulling plugs as discussed in the previous chapter, the rate of drop is a bit faster with divers. Unlike pulling plugs which target a steelhead's visual and auditory senses, backtrolling diver and bait adds a scent-driven aspect. This means presentations can be delivered at faster rates. A faster drop also means less wear and tear on the baits.

Diver Options

When it comes to divers carrying bait to where the fish are, there are several ways this can be accomplished. Perhaps the most popular and effective presentation is Luhr Jensen's Jet Diver. This series of deep-reaching divers provides a consistent pull, keeping your bait precisely where you want it. Various size Jet Divers can be used, depending on the depth and speed of water being fished. In shallow waters, a size 10 Jet Diver may suffice, while deeper waters require a larger, deeper pulling Diver in the 40 to 50 size range.

Plugs are also very effective when used as divers and can

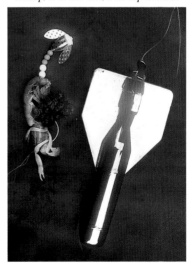

In fast, heavy steelhead water, a Jet Diver is an excellent way of presenting a sand shrimp, or in this case, a shrimp cocktail.

increase the action on a bait. Mud Bugs are my favorite plug, though the proper sizes can be tough to find. There are some tackle shops throughout the West who may have the one-ounce, 4 1/4-inch and 3/4-ounce, 4 1/2-inch Mud Bugs stockpiled in their storage rooms, but it will take some looking to find them as they are no longer in production. The deep-diving ability of these larger Mud Bugs are preferable in higher, fast moving steelheading waters. For lower, summer level streams, Cabela's carries both the 1/4-ounce, 3-inch and 5/8-ounce, 3 1/2-inch Mud Bugs that work well. Along with their built-in rattle, the ability of Mud Bugs to run true and dig down makes them a real workhorse in steelhead waters. Magnum Wiggle Warts and Hot-n-Tots also work well and should not be neglected when considering pulling plugs to get your bait down.

When using plugs as divers, there is no use for hooks. Remove both sets of hooks and paint the bodies black. A flat black coating discourages fish from striking the plugs. When attaching these plugs to the mainline and leader, there are two ways to do it: Tying directly into the eyes of the plug, or using a slider system.

If affixing both lines directly to the plug, the leader is tied into the bottom, or belly eyescrew, while the mainline is attached to the upper, or bill eyescrew. If there are two eyescrews present on the bottom of your plug, tie the leader on the back, trailing eye. This style maximizes movement of the bait and is ideal when pulling plugs with action.

If opting for a slider system, it's set up just as a Jet Diver would be. A slider keeps the plug moving freely on your mainline, a feature I like when working through boulder patches and along turbulent ledges. A slider can easily be made by running a barrel swivel up the mainline, and a bead below that. Tie a 12-inch leader to the swivel, to which is attached the plug/diver. The bead keeps the sliding swivel from wearing on the knot of the mainline. Both the mainline and leader are tied to another barrel swivel. I like this setup when pulling Mud Bugs, for it accentuates their deep diving ability.

Painting a Mud Bug flat black ensures false strikes won't occur on the hookless plug.

Leader & Bait

When fishing diver and bait, leader length can range from three to eight feet. Five- to six-foot-long leaders are a good medium, as that seems to distance the bait far enough from the plug, while at the same time keeping the bait in line. As with all leaders, a quality fluorocarbon can provide a distinct advantage in clear waters.

The beauty of working a diver is that it allows you to slip natural bait into water that might not otherwise receive such a presentation. Eggs, sand shrimp, a shrimp cocktail, and prawns are all good steelhead baits to be pulled by divers. The shrimp cocktail is a favorite of mine, as steelhead often find this combination irresistible. **Because fish tend to swallow these baits extremely deep, avoid using them in rivers with a high percentage of native fish requiring release.**

A drift bobber to fit the size of bait and hook being used is also an important element. While Corkies, Cheaters, Pills and Wobble-Glos are effective, I like a spinning drift bobber for added movement. Spin-N-Glos are excellent, but a preferred trick, taught to me by good friend and Alaskan Guide, Brett Gesh, is to use a Flashing and Spinning Cheater with one clipped wing. When one of the stiff, metallic mylar wings is clipped, the other wing causes an exaggerated spinning effect on the bobber. This added action appears to entice more bites as fish will move a greater distance to attack the flashing, crippled object.

Though more popular among salmon anglers and winter steelheaders, pulling a diver and bait does have a place in summer steelhead fishing. Once you develop a feel for this style, you'll be surprised how often you catch yourself wanting to put it to practice.

A one-winged Flashing and Spinning Cheater created the ideal movement that enticed this fish to bite. Varying your gear can make a difference when it comes to making fish strike.

Chapter 12
Hitting High, Turbid Waters

*E*arly in the season, or following periods of heavy rain, many steelhead anglers stow their rods until water levels and visibility return to what they deem fishable quality. I too used to think this way, until I grew tired of waiting. Rain in the Pacific Northwest can turn rivers off and on well into June, meaning anglers can procrastinate two to three months of good fishing.

Don't let turbid, high waters keep you from fishing; rather, alter your approach and take to the river. One summer steelhead outing into rough waters found me at my highest level of skepticism. We'd been routinely catching fish in rivers with two-and-a-half feet of visibility, but following a rain, that distance diminished to 15-inches. Increasing the size of our terminal to 3/0 Gamakatsu hooks, a large sand shrimp, and a size 6 metallic silver Spin-N-Glo, my buddy and I still managed to nail two nice steelhead.

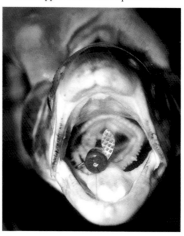
Taken in high, turbid waters with a mere 15 inches of visibility, this steelie inhaled a 3/0 hook topped with a size 6 Spin-N-Glo.

Dealing With The Water
The most difficult aspect to overcome when convincing yourself to fish high waters is the appearance of the river. Because the water looks ugly, spirits often drop and confidence wanes. Not only does this make fishing under such conditions less appealing, it leaves room for doubt in one's mind, and any level of doubt in a fisherman's head is a hindrance.

If you find yourself battling feelings of ambivalence, think about what you know and work from there. You've already done your homework, tracking fish counts over ladders and into local hatchery recycling ponds, so you know fish are in the system. You also know the sense of smell of a steelhead is measured in parts per billion. The only other factor is figuring where the fish are within any given body of water.

Due to increased readings on the turbidimeter, fishing by sight is virtually out of the question. You can always stick to the spots you normally fish in any given fishing hole, but even this act leaves room for question. Because of increased turbulence, steelhead won't necessarily hold in the same places they do when the water is three to five feet lower. Knowing where steelhead hold and move to in high waters are the most important factors when it comes to catching them. It's up to you to put the bait in a place where they can find it.

One such example of knowing where fish hold is vividly etched in my mind. One day in early May, upwards of 30 boats should have been on the river, but there were only four. High waters and low visibility had anglers turned off, but everyone knew fish were in the river. While we drifted bobber and jigs along the shore, two guide boats went by us, one working plugs, the other diver and bait. Both boats ran through the middle of the river, exactly where you'd expect to find steelhead if the water was four feet lower. Neither boat touched a fish.

We followed, but stuck close to the bank, dropping Mud Bugs and shrimp in waters that hadn't been fished. We picked up one bright fish and lost another.

Working from a boat is a productive and very efficient way to cover high, off-color water. Here, this boat is running three diver-and-bait setups, covering lots of water.

With so much water roaring by, steelhead will opt for calmer, less taxing travel routes. They'll move into the shallow, less forceful waters to conserve energy. Knowing this is critical to success.

Many bank anglers I've observed fishing for steelhead in high waters, often wade into where the fish are traveling, inevitably fishing over the steelhead. Had they stood on the bank and worked the mild-flowing waters ten feet in front of them, they would have caught fish.

When figuring out where to find steelhead in high, opaque waters, think of where you'd most likely find trout. This is where you'll want to focus for steelhead.

The Approach

Given the restricted level of visibility and the fact the river is moving at a considerable rate, the objective is to present a bait the fish can see, smell, and have time to grab. This means larger than normal terminal gear and slowing down the presentation so the fish have time to react before it disappears from sight.

If I had one method of fishing steelhead in unfavorable conditions, it would be backtrolling diver and bait. This approach allows you to move slowly downstream, working a large bait at a constant depth, putting it precisely where the fish are. Control is the key, and this must be optimized to consistently take fish amid adverse conditions.

Hooks of 2/0 size are as low as I'll go, with 3/0 hooks being preferred. Both hooks can be covered with an adult sand shrimp, while the extra gap in larger hooks increases your bite-to-catch ratio. Atop the leader, I'll run two to five 3mm beads, stacked above the eye of the hook. Between the beads and the eye, yarn is tied. Beau Mac's Glow Yarn is a good choice, as are fluorescent red, pink, orange and chartreuse colors. The brighter the presentation the better.

Above the beads I prefer a size 6 Flashing and Spinning Cheater or a size 6 Spin-N-Glo. If simultaneously working waters where salmon may be, I've gone up to a size 4, and steelhead have taken them. Metallic or bright bodies coupled with silver mylar wings are favorites. These waters are so opaque, using dark colored attractants are not as effective for the simple reason too much sunlight is blocked by the silt, impeding the silhouette effect that typically results. Luminous Corkies charged with a camera flash or flashlight can also be effective in attracting the attention of fish in off-colored. Luhr Jensen's K-13 Lighted Kwikfish can also catch steelhead in turbid waters.

While working diver and bait gets you into waters that can be difficult to drift fish—and is easier on your bait than casting into turbulent waters—don't overlook casting baits. Hitting the slots closer to shore, from the bank or the opposite side of the river if in a boat, can be very productive. If casting repeatedly in high waters, the addition of scents can be a big help. Smelly Jelly, Pro-Cure and Atlas Mike's all make scents that have increased the success rates of anglers, and finding which ones work in the high, clouded waters you fish can dramatically increase your catch. Incidentally, the hollow bodies sand shrimp acquire after a few casts make great scent chambers, while Luhr-Jensen's Bob Tail rubber egg also is equipped with this feature.

In addition to scents, I like throwing a shrimp cocktail into poor water conditions. Not only does the smell of the eggs attract fish, but the red or orange hue nicely complements a sand shrimp. In addition, the eggs are capable of taking more of a beating than a shrimp.

When fishing eggs by themselves, I've had good luck varying the hook coloration. Gamakatsu's pink and chartreuse hook finishes are bright, captivating colors that I believe play a role in gaining the attention of steelhead. Because steelhead are more reactive to biting visual stimuli than say, salmon, I feel it imperative to work every bit of coloration into my presentation as possible.

Mack's Lures Smile Blades are also good on high water steelhead. These stiff, metallic Mylar blades capture and reflect great amounts of light in murky water. Threaded atop a few beads or a small Cheater or Corky, giving these blades enough room to work is key. They are fished just like any drift bobber setup.

A final approach that has produced steelhead in elevated water conditions is working a collared Stuart Steelhead Bullet. This jig is designed for fishing plastic worms beneath it, and the color combination of the jig and the worm together make a visually appealing presentation. Early one spring a buddy used these jigs, tipped with a six-inch orange worm, to nab several steelhead from a murky river. Others on the same river had luck using a four-inch pink worm. Fished below a bobber, as described in Chapter 6, these unique jigs can produce fish in agitated waters.

If you know fish are in the river and you find yourself mulling over the prospects of wetting a line, don't hesitate. This especially holds true following a rain, when a freshet puts fish on the move, yet often leads to discolored waters. By altering your approach and taking to the river with an open mind, you may be surprised at what can be done.

A size 6 Flashing and Spinning Cheater with a full sand shrimp threaded on a 3/0 hook was not overkill in the high waters from which this fish came. The entire setup is quite large, but this average-sized steelhead didn't hesistate in attacking.

Chapter 13
Tying Your Own Leaders

When it comes to hooks and leaders, you can either purchase pre-tied, snelled hooks, or tie your own. For your time and money, tying your own hooks is the way to go and is surprisingly simple.

The incentives for tying your own hooks before hitting the water are the time saved retying terminal gear that is lost, and the fact that riggings can be customized to your liking. If you have your leaders, complete with yarn, tied and ready to go, you'll significantly increase your fishing time. The last thing you want to do is waste time tying leaders from scratch when you should be fishing; in the five minutes it takes to do so, many fish can scoot by.

Having the option of pre-tied hooks ready to go at all times is a critical step in steelheading preparations. The author prefers varying hook sizes and yarn color, allowing him to match river conditions wherever he may go.

The Hooks

Successful fishing begins with a sharp hook. If the hooks aren't sharp, the odds of catching fish dramatically decreases. Obtain the sharpest hook you can, either through direct purchase or by filing it yourself. Economical hooks can be purchased and sharpened, but these don't hold an edge like fine machined, strong tensile strength hooks. Bottom line, buy the best hook you can afford.

There are many quality hooks on the market, several of which hold an edge after repeated bottom-pounding casts. If dulled through repeated casting, these hooks nicely regain their edge when passed over a Luhr Jensen hook file. Cheaper hooks tend to lose their dagger shape more quickly, rendering them ineffective.

Gamakatsu hooks are tough to beat for the money. While there are more expensive hooks on the market, Gamakatsu brand offers overall effectiveness that's tough to match. Granted, Gamakatsu hooks are a bit on the high end, cost wise, but I've been extremely pleased with their durability and the ease with which they can be sharpened. Search around, try various brands and see what works best for you. If you're losing piles of gear, chances are you'll want to find an affordable hook; but whatever you do, don't sacrifice quality when it costs you fish.

For most summer steelhead fishing, hooks ranging from size 2 to 2/0 are ideal. In extremely low, clear water conditions such as those found in tiny tributaries, size 4 and even size 6 hooks may be used. Accordingly, in high waters I've gone to 3/0 hooks with large drift bobbers and had no trouble hooking steelhead.

The Leader

Leader length is determined by water conditions and fishing regulations. Regulations in many states govern how long a leader you can use. A good rule of thumb is: The shorter the leader, the better. A short leader offers better angler control, meaning you can place the bait precisely where you want it.

But short leaders are not always the best. In clear waters, a compact terminal gear setup may spook fish. In this scenario, a longer leader in the 30- to 36-inch class is good for distancing the bait from the sinker system. Most steelhead leaders I tie are in the 18- to 24-inch range, graduating to the 36-inch mark when I hit clear, mid-summer rivers. If the leader needs to be shortened, it's easy to do while on the river.

During high waters, or when the river is off color, I'll go with 12-pound leader, 10 pound as the very minimum. When rivers clear up and recede to summer levels, I'll drop to 10-pound leader, 8 pound being the lowest weight. These are strong fish, occupying rugged river bottoms. Using line strong enough to hold fish is the objective, not seeing how light of a leader you can get away with, breaking off fish in the process. I once stood by a guy who bragged of hooking many fish that season. While we fished, he hooked four steelhead, breaking off three. He was using 6 pound leader. For the sake of the fish, and my own well being, I'd rather hook three fish and land them all, than hook six and break off half.

On another summer steelhead trip, a guy next to me hooked six nice fish, and broke off every one. Further investigation revealed he was using 8-pound leader, not a good choice in the high, fast water we were fishing. I used 12-pound leader and landed my first two hooked fish.

Proper Storage

Once tied, there are several ways to go about storing leaders. Finished leaders can be wrapped around themselves and placed in baggies or small containers for easy carrying afield, or they can be wrapped on to a section of foam. I've tried both methods, along with several others, and am convinced the best way to go is with a Pip's Hook and Leader Dispenser.

With their array of colors, Pip's Hook & Leader Dispensers are a great way to go. These boxes allow anglers to have a wide variety of hooks tied and ready to fish, and their clear tops make for quick identification of hook size and yarn color.

The Pip's box is the ultimate in storage, as it's easy to use and promotes mobility for bank anglers. Capable of holding plenty of hooks, I typically insert two dozen steelhead leaders per container. The yarn attached to each setup is bulky and I don't like my leaders sitting around for months unused, so I limit the number of leaders stockpiled. I like tying a couple dozen rigs, enough to last a trip or two, and refilling the canister when it's empty.

Ideally, having multiple Pip's containers is the way to go. Available in six colors, I'll use these for organizing various hook sizes, leader length and yarn combinations. With a label placed on the lid, it's easy to keep track of what I have. The clear lids also allow me to see what colors are in store. If I'm going to be bank fishing and want a mix of leaders to meet varied water conditions, I'll pull a blend of leaders from existing containers, place them all in one Pip's box and carry it in my pocket.

Bob Schmidt, Vice President of Mack's Lures, Incorporated, advises anglers using the Pip's boxes to always wind the box clockwise when inserting leaders. "It makes no difference whether or not the leaders are wound in one at a time or all at once," points out Schmidt. "The key when removing a leader is lining up the two slots and pulling the hook out at a 180° angle, directly away from slots. Do not pull toward the slot or in an upward motion. Pulling straight across the lip of the box, being careful not to lift the leader while doing so, will keep the line from slipping into the groove."

It should be noted, large Pip's boxes will soon be on the market. Not only will these boxes accommodate a greater number of hooks, they'll also hold larger hooks with longer leaders.

Egg Loop Knots

I use two types of egg loop knots when tying leaders. The most popular style is the standard egg loop knot, often called the bumper knot. This knot consists of a series of line wraps going evenly down the shank of the hook. The main leader exits from the middle of the wrap and runs through the eye of the hook. Cinched snug, an egg loop is created.

*When pulling leaders from a Pip's box, align both holes and pull flat across the top of
the box, at an 180-degree angle. This will prevent multiple leaders from being uncoiled.*

The egg loop knot is the strongest, sporting a 90% breaking point
strength. I use this when fishing big chinook. But for steelhead, I use the figure 8 egg loop knot, also called the double turle or fly knot. I've heard from
various anglers that this knot's breaking point ranges from 75% to 85% of the
total line strength. All I know is, I've never lost a steelhead due to this knot,
and I use it exclusively on summer runs. I don't regularly use the figure 8 on
other terminal gear, where a direct pull puts stress on the knot. But for an egg
loop, the position of the finished product takes pressure off the knot, dispersing it throughout the line.

I like the figure 8 knot because it's quick to tie, durable and holds the
eggs snugly against the shank of the hook. Three figure 8 egg loops can be
tied in the time it takes to tie one standard egg loop.

Sliding the hook, eye first, on to the leader, let it dangle on the spool
from which you're working. In the left hand, make and hold a large loop, followed by two smaller loops, also pinched between the left thumb and forefinger. Thread the tag end, held in the right hand, through the loops and pull
it tight. As the knot closes, a figure 8 is created. Slide the hook back down the
leader, running the entire hook through the loop. Pull the line snug against
the eye of the hook and you're done.

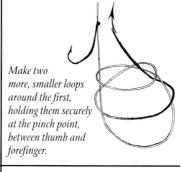

Once mastered, a figure-eight knot is quick and easy, producing mass numbers of leaders. Begin by sliding the hook onto the spool of leader, as shown. Loop the line and pinch between thumb and forefinger at the assigned point.

Make two more, smaller loops around the first, holding them securely at the pinch point, between thumb and forefinger.

Take the tag end of the leader and thread it back through the loops, at the pinch point. To prevent the loops from unraveling, working with a short tag is key.

Pulling the tag end through the loops while holding on to the larger one, the two small loops will

flip over creating a figure-eight. If this design is not acheived, start over. Snugging the knot tight, slide the hook back through the egg loop and snip the leader to desired length.

Adding Yarn

Whichever knot you use, adding yarn for coloration is the next step. Yarn can be tied in the egg loop or above the eye of the hook, on the leader. Tying yarn in the egg loop helps prevent the bait from being severed when the leader is pulled taut. Affixing yarn above the hook, it drapes down over the hook and bait, creating a nice presentation.

I like tying a variety of colored yarns on my leaders, alone or in combination. This allows me to modify my presentation at any given point. When I hit the river, I have leaders tied with, say, orange, pink, and white yarn, as well as a mixed

There are various ways to attach yarn to your leader: between the drift bobber and hook (left), in the egg loop (middle), or above the drift bobber. This is a personal choice, though each method has its devout following of anglers.

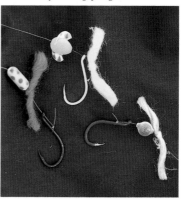

supply of pink and white, black and green, or whatever color combination I desire.

Yarn can be so effective, that many anglers choose to fish it with no bait at all. This is because steelhead are protective of the area they occupy. Debris floating toward a steelhead is often grabbed in the mouth and spit out. Fibers within yarn can catch on the small teeth of steelhead, keeping the hook in their mouth for a precious second or two longer. This may be all the extra time needed for an angler to detect a bite and set the hook.

By pre-tying leaders before heading afield, you're ultimately maximizing fishing time. Bottom line, the more time you spend with your hook in the water, the greater the chances of catching fish. Creating your own leaders and color combinations of yarn is not only rewarding, it's an integral part of the sport. The more you know about each and every aspect of steelhead fishing, the better all-around angler you'll be.

A) A size 2 (left) and 2/0 hook showing a proper match between hook and drift bobber size. Be sure your drift bobber is not too big so as to cover the gap of the hook. B) The author pulled this rigging from the bottom of a popular steelhead hole. Not only is the treble hook a poor choice, but the Corky covers the entire bite of the hook. A larger, single hook is what's needed here.

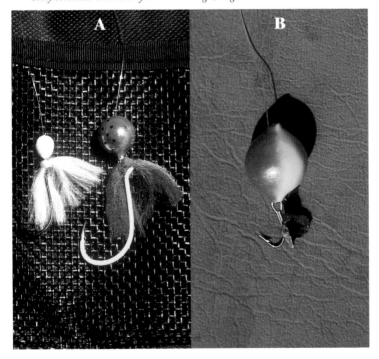

Chapter 14
Egg Cures for Summer Steelhead

The best natural bait for summer steelhead is the egg, or roe. Be it single eggs or clusters, steelhead love feeding on them. The key is finding a good egg that steelhead can see, smell and taste. Because we are dealing with fast water fishing, obtaining a bait that withstands turbid waters, holds up cast after cast, and retains its color are critical points.

The Primary Goals

Due to the fact most steelhead fishing with eggs takes place in fast water, many anglers consider taste to be the primary target in a good bait. If you think about it, it makes sense. Casting into rapids puts a certain amount of bow in your line. While it may seem you're nearing the bottom of a drift, your terminal gear may only be halfway through the run. Should a steelhead grab it, chances are you won't immediately feel it. For this reason alone, it's important to present a bait steelhead like the taste of and will hold in their mouth.

If you've ever watched a steelhead bite eggs, you know what I mean. I've seen steelhead literally pick my eggs clean, while I didn't feel a single twinge on the line. I've also watched them swallow my eggs, only to spit them out with my not even sensing the bite.

I consider sight to be the second most important factor in a good egg cure. Because steelhead have superior vision, they have the ability to detect minute particles floating downstream. A good color combination of eggs, yarn, and a drift bobber of choice can mean the difference in making a fish move, wanting to bite, or remaining closed-mouth. This is why many anglers prefer bright orange, pink or red dyed eggs. Milked out, flesh color combinations can also be good attention getters.

Because many steelhead survive after spawning, they have a feeding instinct upon entering a river. Due to this fact, they are much more likely to strike than say, salmon. Knowing this means steelhead are not too picky about what they attack, which is why serving the sense of sight is second in my book.

Smell would rank third on my list of priorities when trying to achieve a good steelhead cure. Unlike salmon, steelhead are not chemical junkies. They don't crave the same mineral contents as salmon, so cures carrying less chemical scents are often used on steelhead.

In addition, steelhead typically sought by egg fishermen are in fast water, where milking contents and the smell of scents are swiftly carried downstream. Mind you, this does not mean scents should be neglected. I use them religiously, both in my cures and on the river.

Be it generic or dyed, borax is great for curing summer steelhead fishing eggs.

Borax Cures

Due to their ability to harden eggs, borax cures are popular among anglers looking to cure egg clusters. In addition, borax cures are clean and easy to work with. There are two options when searching for borax cures: Commercial products and homespun recipes.

Pro-Cure has a variety of borax cures on the market, ranging from natural to flame orange and fluorescent pink. I've used these cures and they turn out a very good egg.

Atlas-Mike's also has a borax cure called Alaska Premier Bait. Both their radiant and natural colors are popular and produce good-looking eggs.

Many home recipes call for powdered borax, a box of which can be purchased at most grocery stores. If working with this type of borax, be sure to get the non-scented powder form, not the course-grained variety. The finer the grains, the more completely they will react with the eggs to make a better cure.

The colored borax cures on the market already have dyes in them. The purpose is for the egg tissue to absorb this dye, creating a color that's attractive to steelhead. If the color of the finished product is not what you envisioned, you can introduce dyes.

From red food coloring to commercial products, there are a variety of ways to dye eggs. The most effective dyes I've used are created by Beau Mac Enterprises. Both their Pro Glow Bait Coloring and their Instant Bait Color work very well. The Instant Bait Color can be applied to eggs that lose luster when on the river, while the Bait Coloring is introduced during the curing process. Both create vivid results that capture a steelhead's attention.

If it's the natural look you're after, no dyes need to be applied. A natural-looking egg can be obtained by working with some of the prepackaged, natural-colored cures on the market or by concocting your own recipe.

Beau Mac has a series of dyes that are excellent for putting color in eggs. This bait was nearly flesh color but was brought back to life with orange bait coloring.

Chemical-Based Cures

Chemical bases are commonly found in most commercial cures on the market. They are aptly applied to eggs intended for salmon fishing, though there are anglers who rely on them to catch steelhead. One of my favorite steelhead fishing cures calls for sodium bisulfite.

Sulfites and sulfates are a salt or ester of sulfurous acid or sulfuric acid, respectively. Vegetable and animal fats are examples of esters. Esters usually have pleasant odors and are the reason for the appealing aroma in many fruits and flowers. These smells attract fish to eggs cured with sulfites and sulfates. Nitrates and nitrites also hold chemical properties similar to one another.

While eggs cured for salmon may employ a great deal of nitrates, nitrites, sulfates or sulfites, steelhead cures should be toned down. Be careful not to introduce the wrong scent or overdo it with any one particular chemical, for fear of driving off steelhead.

These chemical cures milk out well, releasing a great deal of scent into the water. They are very good cures for adding scents to, especially during the curing process. When curing, eggs exposed to any one of these chemicals undergo osmosis and plasmolysis, where water moves in and out of the cells. During the stage of reabsorption—

Adding scent to a bait can make the difference between catching fish or not. The author has found this particularly true when sight-fishing for finicky steelhead.

where eggs soak up the water initially released in the curing process—scents and dyes make their way into the tissue and membranes within the skein. This is a major benefit of chemical cures.

There are several scents on the market, and anglers willing to experiment with them typically increase their odds of catching fish. In many of the cures I've used on steelhead, be it chemical or borax, I've had very good success with Pro-Cure, Smelly Jelly and Atlas-Mike's scents.

The Curing Process

Obtaining a particularly well cured egg begins the moment you catch a hen. After pictures have been snapped, kill the fish with a blow to the head. Once dead, bleed it by cutting the gills or ringing the underside of the tail. Bleeding a fish soon after death allows the blood to be pumped from the body.

The quicker you can get the blood out of a fish, the less likely it is to pool around organs. Blood that pools and coagulates around the eggs results in exposure to bacteria, organisms that will taint the smell of eggs and decrease their effectiveness no matter what curing recipe is used.

Some anglers forego the bleeding, opting to immediately remove the eggs from the fish instead. Others go so far as to remove the eggs with rubber gloves on, to avoid contaminating them with human odors. Blotting the skeins with a paper towel removes blood that may harbor bacteria. Placing the skeins in a baggie and in a cooler is ideal if you're set on removing the eggs, usually a wise choice on hot days.

Whether you transport the eggs in the fish or in baggies, make certain when extracting the skeins you don't cut too deep. With the fish on its back, make a small incision at the anus, just big enough to insert two fingers. With these two fingers side-by-side, lift up on the belly, slipping a short-bladed knife between them and cut upwards. Avoid deep cuts, for fear of damaging the membrane that holds the eggs together.

Starting with a clean, blood-free skein of eggs is the first step in attaining the perfect bait.

Once home and ready to cure, I like cutting my skeins into bait sizes I know I'll use when fishing for steelhead. I do this for two reasons: I believe it allows them to more completely set up during the curing process and I don't have to spend time cutting them to bait size when I'm fishing.

When you begin cutting your eggs, make certain enough membrane is attached to each bait so they will remain intact when placed on the hook. The less membrane, the shorter the casting life and the less effective they will be.

If using a store-bought cure, follow the instructions to obtain the best results. If using a homemade recipe, be sure to rotate the eggs once or twice a day to ensure the ingredients are making their way into the eggs.

Once removed from the cure, air drying is a vital step in securing a quality finished product. Remove each bait from the cure and place them on racks or paper towels. Avoid sunlight coming in contact with the eggs; a shaded area is ideal. On warm, summer days, drying time may only be a matter of minutes. In cool, moist or warm, humid environments, drying may take a day or two. Some folks will position an electric fan over the eggs to expedite drying.

The objective of air drying is to achieve a firm egg that will resist punishment delivered in fast moving steelhead waters. Attention must be paid so the eggs don't dry to the point they become too dry and are severed when your egg loop is cinched tight. As a rule of thumb, I prefer eggs that are dried to the point that when I squeeze them between my thumb and forefinger, they retain that shape. I don't like them so soft they return to their original shape, nor so hard they crack when squeezed.

Proper Storage

Once the eggs are cured, I place two to three dozen baits in a baggie. This is approximately the number I'll use during a day of fishing. If I'm going to be gone all day, I'll toss a few more baggies of baits in a cooler.

When on the river, take extreme care to keep your eggs in a cool, shaded area. Sunlight hitting the eggs will darken them and ruin the texture, greatly inhibiting their fish-catching ability. This can be challenging during the hot summer months. If fishing from a river boat, a cooler is the ideal location to store eggs not in use. If bank fishing, you may want to carry a little cooler along, or keep one in the truck if you don't want to haul it around the river.

The baggie of eggs I'm fishing with will be kept in a bait box or plastic container. If I'm bank fishing, the bait box will be attached to my belt, lid shut, ensuring sunlight does not reach the eggs. If in a boat, I'll place the eggs I'm fishing with in a plastic container, keeping them in the shadow of a tackle box or beneath a towel on the floor.

The eggs I'm not using will be kept in the refrigerator or a freezer. If I know I'm going to use them over the course of the next month, I'll leave them in baggies in the refrigerator. But, if I have a healthy supply of eggs, I'll keep them in the freezer for up to a year. If your freezer creates a lot of moisture, it's a good idea to pack the eggs in borax to retard against freezer burn.

To learn more about egg cures, refer to my book, *Egg Cures: Proven Recipes and Techniques*. This book offers more than two dozen recipes, includes egg handling tips, and outlines how to cure cluster and single eggs. It can be ordered through Frank Amato Publications.

Chapter 15
Gathering Baits

In addition to roe, there are other natural baits that steelhead find particularly attractive. While these range from insect larvae to deep sea creatures, we're going to consider the three most available to the average angler. If you have a bit of extra time on your hands, are looking to save some money, or simply want to be responsible for acquiring as many of your own fishing accessories as possible, consider gathering your own baits.

Sand shrimp, worms and crawdads are baits steelhead love, and gathering them can be nearly as fun as fishing; well, almost.

Sand Shrimp

Sand, or ghost, shrimp are one of the most favored steelhead baits of all. A mainstay in a steelhead's diet while in the ocean, sand shrimp are no less tantalizing when presented in fast water conditions. Due to their color, scent, or a combination of the two, there's no doubt, sand shrimp can draw strikes when nothing else will.

Obtaining sand shrimp is a joy in itself, and is a great opportunity to take the family on an ocean getaway. Most Pacific Northwest coastal bays hold sand shrimp, though some can be better than others. To learn of shrimp abundance near where you intend to dig, calling a fish and game office is recommended prior to heading out. They can provide helpful information in terms of where to go and what to expect.

Digging your own sand shrimp can be very economical. Here, just over 100 dozen shrimp were pumped, leading to several days of good fishing.

Hitting the low tides provides good shrimping, but minus tides produce the best conditions. Search for pencil-sized holes in the sand—the more you can locate, the better. Hopefully you'll find an area so riddled with shrimp holes, you can't take a step in any direction without covering several. Clam guns are the way to go, as digging with a shovel is not efficient. In one pull it's common to retain multiple shrimp, sending you home with scores of crustaceans in just a few hours of pumping.

If serious about shrimping, perhaps you can acquire or build your own shrimp gun, the results of which will pay huge dividends. Using 3 feet of 2-inch-diameter PVC pipe, with a hand-drawn plunger that creates a vacuum, the idea is to delve deeper than what a standard clam gun reaches. A narrower shrimp gun also takes the pressure off lifting so much sand, as is the case with a clam gun. If buying a clam gun, purchase the narrowest cylinder you can find, or better yet, invest in a specially made shrimp gun that can be purchased at select coastal marinas and tackle shops.

There are several ways to handle your shrimp once home. If you're lucky and live near the ocean, keeping them alive in a large cooler of saltwater is no problem. Changing the water each day assures they stay fresh and lively. They can be kept for several days, even weeks, if cared for properly. If you don't have access to saltwater, tropical fish and aquarium stores have chemicals that can be added to tap water, creating a saltwater environment. These chemicals take a few days to balance out, and should be prepared prior to digging. An aerator or a saltwater filter can also be added, greatly enhancing the life of your shrimp.

If you don't live near the ocean, yet want to keep shrimp alive, you can transport them home in a cooler. Place blocks of ice in the bottom so no cracks exist, and cover them with several layers of newspaper; this will keep the shrimp until you get home. The key is to keep the shrimp from coming into contact with fresh water, which causes them to urinate on themselves and spoil. Atop the newspaper, put down a few layers of paper towels and dampen with saltwater. Spread your shrimp over the toweling, covering them with a few more layers of damp paper towels. This will keep them clean and cool. Once home, change out the paper towels for fresh, dry ones. I've kept shrimp alive for up to ten days in this way, but they do require a great deal of care. The water needs to be regularly drained from the cooler and the ice must be changed every two to three days to ensure the shrimp do not come into contact with fresh water. If they contact fresh water, they will die and turn soft.

Storing shrimp in the refrigerator is another option. Using the large kind of wood chips sold for dog or hamster bedding, place a few inches in a styrofoam cup. Add a dozen or so shrimp and affix the lid. Many anglers prefer this method for keeping shrimp alive, as it requires less effort and if some die, at least the entire batch won't go bad, only what's in that carton. Keeping the shrimp cool, in the 40- to 45-degree range, will slow their metabolism and extend their life.

While live shrimp are tougher than frozen specimens, withstanding considerably more punishment when fished in turbulent waters, many people choose to freeze them right away. If you know you won't be hitting the river enough to use up your cache of live shrimp, freezing them is a good idea. If freezing the shrimp, transport them home in a cooler of saltwater. (Again, keeping shrimp in the natural saltwater prevents them from spoiling due to the toxins in their urine.) Once home, remove the shrimp by hand, blot them dry and place in the containers in which they'll be frozen. Freezing a dozen or two per container is good, as more than that will prolong the thawing process. You can also place a desired number of shrimp in baggies, cover them with saltwater, and freeze. Some anglers freeze shrimp in Karo syrup.

When thawing shrimp, allow it to take place naturally, at room temperature. Resist the urge to run them under hot water, or thaw in the microwave, for fear too much softening will occur. It's best to take them out the night before fishing. If they're not thawed when you hit the river, pan water over them to expedite things.

The high water content inside a shrimp makes it an ideal scent chamber, while simultaneously retaining lifelike color. When frozen and thawed for fishing, sand shrimp entrails shrink, creating plenty of space for scents to be injected. When fished live, to the point most of the entrails disintegrate, a scent chamber is also produced within the shrimp.

Fished alone, or in combination with drift bobbers, the presentation of shrimp can be deadly on summer steelhead. If eggs, lures or plugs aren't producing, changing to shrimp can be the ticket to success.

Small and medium shrimp can be fished whole, with only the large, white pincer being removed. On large shrimp, the tail and carapace can be split in half, with both sections being fishable baits. Many anglers opt to use only the tail, with or without a drift bobber of choice.

When it comes to attaching a whole shrimp, I like running the hook completely through the tail, through the abdomen, and burying it into the carapace with the point protruding. The tail and abdomen can be slid over the eye of the hook and up on the leader. A half-hitch can then be looped around the tail, firmly securing the shrimp in an upright position. This technique allows the shrimp to lay out flat, and it stays on very well.

A commercial threader allows a shrimp to be easily slid over the hook, onto the leader. Running the shrimp headfirst onto the threader, slide it on the hook, tail first. Slide the shrimp up the hook, onto the leader, until the mouth comes to rest in the curve of the hook. Run the egg loop around the shrimp or throw a half-hitch around its tail and you're set. Some anglers go the extra step by tying a small piece of thread around the shrimp and hook

Commercial shrimp threaders (left) are popular for affixing a bait. But threading them by hand also works (right). Running the hook through the tail, abdomen and under side of the carapace, then throwing a half-hitch around the tail, the shrimp stays on in even the fastest steelhead water.

to help hold it on, but I've found the egg loop or half-hitch to suffice and be easier to work with.

If you go through a high volume of sand shrimp, purchasing them at $2.75 a dozen, it doesn't take long for your digging and preservation efforts to pay off.

Nightcrawlers

Nightcrawlers are excellent steelhead bait and yield good numbers of fish each summer. They can be fished whole, which is the way many anglers prefer, or cut in half. Half of a nightcrawler however, can be too inviting for trout, and contrary to popular belief, steelhead rarely, if ever, strike short on a whole night crawler; they inhale the bait, hook and all.

That's not to say half a nightcrawler won't work. If in waters void of trout, the head-end of nightcrawlers are very effective. Topped with a drift bobber of choice, this can produce fish when nothing else will. Testing baits one summer day, I fished fresh water shrimp, my dad fished eggs and our buddy, Russ Mathews, fished half a nightcrawler topped with a pair of size 12 Patriot Corkies. Russ nailed five steelhead before Dad and I had a nibble. It was midday and 90°, the sun was directly on the water and the metallic Corkies obviously appealed to the fish. While Dad and I used the same

Patriot Corkies, it was the worm that proved to be the key element. Be it the smell of the earthworm, the movement it carried when drifted, the silhouette appearance it gave off, or all three in combination, there's no doubt half of a worm was the way to go on this day.

Nightcrawlers fished whole or in halves can prove deadly on steelhead when nothing else seems to work.

Finding nightcrawlers during the spring is easy, as rainfall keeps the ground moist and worms active at night. When the air temperature dips below 47° worms become inactive, so I avoid picking on cool nights. While lawns may be tough to find worms in, search for exposed dirt areas to find the most worms. Orchards are a favorite place for worms, and picking a couple thousand in a night is common. These were the numbers I was pulling when I was a kid, selling worms to regional distributors. Crop fields and pastures where grasses are short early in the spring are also ideal worm hangouts.

During the dry summer months, search baseball fields, crop fields, irrigated orchards, tilled ground and well manicured lawns such as golf courses. Any place that receives irrigation on a regular basis is capable of holding worms.

If you want to save your back by not picking worms every time you wish to go fishing, there's the option of picking several in one night and keeping them alive in worm boxes. There are several commercial worm boxes on the market, designed to keep worms alive for extended periods of time. Purchasing commercial worm bedding is also a good choice. Follow the directions to determine proper water content and feeding needs. Some bedding comes complete with supplemental food.

If you wish to make your own worm box, one can be constructed from scrap lumber materials. My grandfather had a large, 3x6 foot box he built and kept worms in for years. Soaking shredded newspapers, squeeze the water out until it quits dripping. This material will account for at about 75% of the bedding. The remainder of the bedding consists of quality soil. Corn meal and coffee grounds can occasionally be sprinkled on top for food.

No matter what size your worm box, keep it cool at all times. Small boxes can simply be kept in a refrigerator; larger ones in a basement or cool corner of a garage. The cooler temperature slows the worm's metabolism, keeping them alive and healthy longer.

When adding freshly picked worms to your box, don't mix them into the soil unless they're going to be fished in the next day or two. If you have a large worm box you intend to use for years, gently spread your catch over the surface. Healthy worms will work their way down into the soil. Injured worms—those incurring internal harm from damaging one of their multiple hearts or a vein—will remain on the surface and should be discarded. Never put halves of worms in the box hoping they will regenerate; it's not worth having them die, molding and contaminating the rest of your stock.

The more lively your nightcrawler, the more tantalizing the presentation. Fished whole, representing worms that have fallen into a stream, steelhead will often hit this natural bait when other baits draw no response. Topped with a size 14 Spin-N-Glo or size 10 Flashing and Spinning Cheater, lifelike action is imparted on the worm. Pills are also effective attractants that nicely compliment a worm's shape.

Crawdads

Crawdads, or crayfish as they're often referred to, are good, scent-rich baits steelhead love. One theory as to why steelhead strike crawdads so vigorously stems from the steelhead's urge to remove impediments that come into their line of sight. During the spawn, crawdads will often invade steelhead redds, and the protective fish have routinely been observed tearing crawdads apart. Whether the smell of crawdads triggers an aggressive response, or if the strike comes as a result of a well-placed cast, is hard to say. But, some rivers do appear to yield more steelhead on crawdad tails than others.

Crawfish can wreak havoc on steelhead redds, they make good bait as adult steelhead despise them.

Gathering crawdads can be another one of those family fun outings. In the summer, when water levels have dropped, wading into streams, gigging crawdads is a ball. I like wading my way down a stream, dropping nylon stockings filled with baits along the way. On my return upstream, I'll spear or dip net what crawdads are near the bait, gathering the nylons as I go.

There are also commercial crawdad traps available. Traps are slick if you live near a stream and don't have the time to devote to gigging. However you go about harvesting crawdads, be aware of daily and possession limits within respective streams or states.

Due to a crawdad's size, tails are typically the only part that is fished. They are best used fresh, in fact, I like taking them to the river alive, then pealing off the tails as needed. The meat from crawdad tails can be toughened-up by placing them in a microwave for one minute before leaving home. Sacrificing natural oil loss for firmness is a judgment call on your part. There is also the option of cooking the tail, then adding crawdad scent to the meat. There are several proven crawfish scents on the market.

Crawdad tails can be threaded onto the hook, then secured in an egg loop, or simply placed in an egg loop if the tail section is large enough. Topped with any drift bobber to match the fishing conditions, and some pink or orange yarn, this is a natural bait that receives too little attention.

With all three of these natural baits, it's imperative to cast using your entire arm, rather than whipping your wrist as when tossing eggs or lures. A big, sweeping cast imparts a constant centripetal force throughout the duration of the cast, keeping baits intact. The more gentle your casts, the longer the fishing life of these baits.

Bay, Freshwater and Dyed Shrimp

While on the topic of natural baits, freshwater shrimp and bay, or salad, shrimp need recognition. Both types of shrimp can be purchased at the local meat counter and can be dyed or fished in their natural state.

On bay shrimp, if fished naturally, putting them in the microwave 30 to 40 seconds prior to leaving home is a good idea. This will firm up the shrimp, allowing them to hold better on the hook. If dying popcorn-size shrimp, air dry or place in the microwave after the dye has set, to firm them up.

Freshwater shrimp is a very effective summer steelhead bait. I like it because it's durable in turbulent waters that might otherwise mutilate a sand shrimp in a few casts. In one such hole, I used purple-dyed freshwater shrimp and outfished my partner four to one on his eggs.

Dying both bay and peeled freshwater shrimp can be done one of two ways: By sprinkling granulated dye over the top or soaking them in a water solution. If the shrimp are fairly juicy, sprinkling dye over them is fast and easy. But be warned, the dye sets rapidly, within a matter of minutes. Whichever color you select, monitor it closely to achieve the desired color. Once the color has been reached, run the shrimp under cold water until it runs clear.

A water-and-dye solution is also effective for dying both shrimp. Make the dye the color you wish and add enough of the solution to cover the shrimp. Again, this can take quickly, don't leave them unattended for too long. If using green or purple dyes, I don't like leaving them in the solution much more than 20 minutes. The time you leave them in the solution depends on the color of the mixture and the end results you want to achieve. When done, rinse under cold, running water until the flow is clear.

If dying sand shrimp is of interest, there's another technique that will help the dye take on these shelled specimens. Make a 100% salt solution by running water through a strainer of rock salt, then add your dye to the pan of water. Be sure to use an old sauce pan for this task, as the dye may be permanent. Bring the solution to a light boil and add your shrimp. Let them boil for a minute or so, to firm them up. Make sure they don't turn too brittle, as this will make fishing with them unfeasible. Strain the solution, saving the dye for future use. Place the shrimp in a 100% cold, saltwater bath for a day or so, to allow them to setup. They're then ready to fish.

Beau Mac specializes in dyes that are tough to beat. Pro-Cure also has a line of dyes which are effective to color shrimp.

If you have the time and desire to gather your own baits, you'll gain a new respect for what this aspect of steelhead fishing entails. In the end, you'll develop a deeper connection with the fish you pursue and the sport we love so much.

Dyed and scented freshwater shrimp and bay shrimp are good bait alternatives that produce fish.

Chapter 16
Do-It-Yourself Sinkers

S teelhead anglers can cut several corners to minimize gear costs. One of the easiest, and most overlooked, is pouring your own sinkers. Be it pencil, bank or slinky sinkers for drift fishing, flat sinkers for plunking, or jig heads you're looking to pour, it can all be done at home.

I've been fishing steelhead since the late 1960s and have never purchased a single sinker to be used on these fish. It's safe to say I've saved thousands of dollars by pouring my own sinkers and jig heads. Not only is it cost-effective, it's fun.

The Setup

With the advent of quality pouring equipment, casting your own sinkers is safe and simple. All that's required is a melting furnace, a few molds, and some lead. If you're pouring jigs, hooks are obviously needed.

These days, lead is fairly easy to get ahold of. Many businesses dealing with lead are forced to unwillingly stockpile the element, thus they are happy to give it away or sell it at a low price. Keeping in mind that softer lead yields better-quality sinkers, check with local plumbing and sheet-metal shops to see what they have available. Lead from these places usually comes in flattened sheets or rolls. Metal dealers, scrap-metal companies, roofing businesses and tire shops are also good sources to inquire about getting recycled lead. Typically, lead from tire shops contains zinc and is quite hard, resulting in brittle sinkers. If possible, mix brittle lead with soft lead to attain a more desirable sinker.

Once you're set up with molds and a pot, pouring your own sinkers is fun, safe and saves loads of cash over the years.

The safest and most effective lead pouring results can be attained through the use of an electric furnace. Cabela's carries two quality electric furnaces. The Production Pot IV, by Lee, handles 10 pounds of lead and heats quickly. For those looking to pour more volume, check out the Mag 20 Electric Furnace, by Lyman. This furnace has a 20-pound capacity.

As for molds, they cost roughly $30 each. The type of fishing you do will determine what molds you need. Some steelheaders may opt for bank, pencil or jig molds. Others may be fans of slinky sinkers, for which the blank cord can be purchased and the round shot sinkers poured. If you're looking for split shots, there are molds for those, too.

Do-It Lure & Sinker Molds have one of the most complete lines of molds for anglers to choose from. These are precision molds that fit tightly, producing high-quality, ready to fish sinkers. Do-It Molds can also be purchased through Cabela's or direct from the Do-It factory. Hilts brand molds are another option and are sometimes available through sporting good stores. Lil' Mac used to make molds, though they can be tough to come by today. I've run across some older model molds at garage sales and secondhand stores.

The Pour

Used wisely, lead is safe to work with. Situate yourself in a well-ventilated area, where fumes can easily escape. If you can't work outside, a shop or garage with all outside doors and windows open is the next best thing. You want air movement near the melting lead to assure fumes aren't concentrated and inhaled.

While pouring sinkers, use gloves to prevent exposure to the skin any time you come in contact with lead. Lead easily rubs off on bare skin and can be absorbed by the body. Eye protection in the form of goggles or a shield should also be worn.

It should be noted that water and lead don't mix. Avoid placing your furnace in the rain or near running water for fear of a potential explosion. If using pipe lead, make sure there are no air pockets. The only close call I had when pouring sinkers was in dealing with some plumber's lead. This lead came in hollow tubes, and I was bending it to fit into my cast-iron melting pot. One of the pieces got an air pocket and burst, sending a stream of lead past my nose, ripping off my baseball cap and pasting the rafters in the garage. I should have taken the time to cut that lead into manageable lengths with a hacksaw.

Plug in the furnace, place the lead in the pot, and start it melting. With the lead melted, heat your molds. A hot mold is essential to producing quality sinkers. You can either heat the molds internally or externally. Internally heating the molds means pouring four to five rounds of lead into the mold before a useable product is attained. If the mold is too cool, lead will stick to the sides, resulting in incomplete or rough-edged sinkers. Externally heating the molds is another option. Placing molds on a Coleman stove, hot plate, even in the oven, will prepare them for casting. No matter how you heat the molds, wear thick gloves when handling them.

The advantage of heating your molds externally is that they seem to retain heat longer, meaning quality pours can be had each time. I like external heat if I'm working with three or four different molds as it allows me to quickly rotate through them. While pouring one and letting another setup, one or two molds remain on the heat source at all times. This is especially efficient if working with a partner, but take care not to move too quickly. If the molds are too hot, sinkers have a tendency to separate when the mold is opened. If this is the case, leave the mold open for a bit, allowing it to cool down before the next pour is made.

With the mold heated and lead melted, you're ready to pour. If using an electric furnace, the handle on the side opens a bottom pour valve. All you have to do is hold the closed mold under it, filling each hole. It's easy to manage two to three molds when working with an electric furnace. When one mold is filled, quickly fill the second and third, then remove the sinkers from each in the order your poured.

Once the sinkers have been removed, immediately close the molds to prevent heat loss. This will ensure the mold stays warm and produces quality sinkers with each pour. A trick that can assist in rapid removal of sinkers from the mold involves a candle. Light the candle and hold it close to the face of your open mold. The soot buildup from the candle will stick to the mold, keeping sinkers from sticking to the molds. Some guys don't like this for the simple reason it chars their molds.

When a pile of sinkers accumulates, clip the sprues—the excess lead attached to the top or bottom of a sinker—from the finished product. In removing the sprues, you can either do it at the end of the pour, or periodically throughout the pouring. If done periodically, the clipped sprues can be placed back in the furnace and remelted. If done at the end, a pile of sprues can be held until the next time you pour, or can be remelted and poured into ingots for easy storage.

Gate shears are available for clipping sprues, giving a nice, even cut. Or you can use wire cutters. Wire cutters often leave a sharp edge on sinkers that can easily be pounded out. Try and remove all sharp edges from your sinkers to prevent line abrasions when fishing.

If your finished sinkers have ragged edges consisting of excess lead, this is a result of offset or rough plates. Make sure the hinges are tight on your mold, yielding a perfect match-up of both sides. A warp-resistant, machined alloy mold is what you want. However, after extended use, even the best molds may result in rough-edged sinkers. Rough-edged sinkers can simply be rubbed or lightly pounded, flattening down edges and making them fishable. In the case of pencil sinkers, a pile can be taken and rolled between your gloved hands, flattening any tattered edges.

Fine-grit abrasive paper can also be taken to the faces of molds. A light sanding should rid the plates of any residue or uneven spots, ensuring the plates fit tight when shut.

Pouring Jigs

More and more anglers are taking to crafting their own jigs. While poured heads and hooks can be bought, you can take it a step further and pour your own. All you need, in addition to that outlined above, are some jig hooks.

The key to successful jig pouring lies in being organized. You need to get the hooks placed in the molds quickly and this can be done by laying out the hooks on a workbench, prior to starting the casting process. If you have tangled bundles of hooks, not only will you encounter punctured fingers in the haste of working quickly, but you'll get flustered at incomplete jig heads, the result of a cool mold.

Lay your hooks out in rows, all facing the same direction so you can quickly grab and place them in the mold. This will assure the mold stays warm and that you achieve the best quality jig heads. Quickly center the eye of each hook in the mold. As the hooks are more efficiently handled with a bare hand, keep in mind the mold is hot. With the hooks in place, carefully close the mold, making sure no gaps are present. If gaps are noticeable, a hook likely jarred from its position.

After pouring each individual jig hole, run the entire mold back and forth under the opened pour valve. This creates a single, sturdy bar across the top of the mold. Once cooled, open the mold and pop the entire slab out, to which is attached the jigs. Now, rather than clipping each jig and sprue, simply grasp the bar and snap each jig off by hand—no snips are needed. Place the bar back into the melting pot and remelt it. This saves a great deal of time due to quick and easy handling.

Slinky Sinkers

Creating slinky sinkers is a cinch. You can buy split-shot or sling-shot pellet molds from Do-It. If using split-shot molds, simply do not insert the separating blade, this will result in a solid, round pellet.

Slinky cord can be purchased at sporting good stores or tackle shops. Buying in bulk is the most cost-effective over the long-term. With the pellets cast, cut the cord to desired lengths. Place one end over a burning candle, melting the fibers, then bind them with a pair of pliers. Dipping the closed end in cold water will harden the seal and cool it down, making it safer for handling.

With one end firmly sealed shut, insert the desired number of pellets. The number of pellets you insert depends on the water you'll be fishing, but

*If you do a lot of fishing, creating your own slinky sinkers
is the way to go, right down to pouring your own shot.*

that's the beauty of crafting your own, you can produce a wide variety of weights allowing you to cover a vast range of water.

With the cord full, heat the other end over the candle, seal it with pliers and dip in water. Once cooled, thread a snap swivel through one end and you're set. When you hit the river all you have to do is thread the weight on your mainline or snap it to a swivel.

Incidentally, if you purchase the slinky chord with white filler inside, don't throw it away. Cut to size, this material can be tied to your hook or leader, giving off a pulsating movement steelhead find attractive. It can be left free to float, resembling a flesh pattern or tied down, to mimic a crawdad. Fished with bait, alone, or with scents, this is an item you'll want in your tackle box.

The Cost Factor

Given the vast selection of sinkers on the market, it's safe to say one sinker costs approximately .50¢. Say you fish 30 days for summer steelhead—or any fish this season—and lose 10 bank sinkers each trip. That's a rough total of $5.00 a day, $150 a season in sinkers. Now total that over a 30-year career. You've just spent $4,500 on sinkers alone.

For under $150 you can acquire most of the supplies needed to pour your own sinkers. Not only is crafting your own sinkers economical when compared to buying ready-made ones, it's enjoyable too. Taking a few hours from a busy schedule once or twice a year to create your own sinkers also adds to the complete arsenal we anglers take pride in. By investing time rather than money, you'll be amazed at how cost-efficient casting your own sinkers can be.

Chapter 17
Record Keeping

You've just landed a steelhead and resume fishing soon after punching your tag. But don't let the writing stop there. Accurate record keeping is something that not only increases your knowledge about steelhead behavior, it can accentuate your total catch. Not only should records reflect fish landed, but also those that have been hooked and lost, strikes, and even days where no nibbles occurred.

By amassing comprehensive records, a reference base soon develops that proves beneficial, starting immediately and lasting a lifetime. Fortunately, Dad encouraged me to keep records beginning at a young age. As a result, I have documentation dating back more than 30 years. It's interesting how vivid in one's mind a fish remains. Even those fish caught 25 years ago seem like yesterday, but the photos and records don't lie.

I like snapping photos of as many fish as I can. Not only does this preserve a lifetime of memories, it provides valuable images in terms of water conditions, quality and size of fish. It's a good idea to jot down some notes while on the river; these need not be lengthy, as you don't want to cut into fishing time, but capture the obvious details.

Taking time to record notes while on the river is one of the best ways to educate yourself on the comprehensive conditions surrounding summer steelhead fishing.

The Gear

What do I possibly record, you might ask? Anything that may be deemed applicable to your catching success. The obvious things that come to mind center around gear. Color, size and style of drift bobber are good starting points, as is the type of bait. Yarn color, if any was used, hook size and color, and even the type of sinker setup and how much weight was used can all be valuable bits of information regarding the use of terminal gear.

Keeping track of what scents were used is also important. I like taking it one step further and documenting the instances where I switched scents, that is, noting what scent didn't work and which one ultimately elicited a bite. This information, combined with natural elements that prevail, pays dividends on future trips.

If using plugs, lures, flies, jigs or diver and bait, reference what exactly it was that produced a strike. When pulling plugs, note what color and size plug it was that drew the hit, and what other plugs were being fished at the time of the strike. Such records will provide conclusive evidence on what plugs work best, and will no doubt influence your becoming attached to a "favorite" plug.

In pulling diver and bait, as in working plugs, note the depth at which you fished. Perhaps the number of times line runs back and forth across the bait-casting reel, typically measured in feet, is the best way to go about it. This will allow you to examine at what depth most of your fish are being hooked, and what adjustments you may need to make to get your presentation down to the proper depth in all river conditions you may face.

When fishing with bobber and jig, note jig size and color, leader length, and how far above the swivel your bobber was (i.e. the depth you were fishing). For flies, note pattern and fishing style. On lures, mark down type, color, size and when the hit occurred, be it on the fall, retrieve, or swing.

The Natural Elements

Aside from the date, name of the river, the hole you hooked a fish in—and even the section of the hole in which it was hooked—there are other natural factors to be aware of. By being cognizant of the natural elements involved in steelhead fishing, anglers become more attuned to fish behaviors, habitat they occupy, and conditions under which success develops. These natural factors may remain constant throughout a day's fishing, or shift several times during the day. Noting such shifts are important.

Environmental factors both above and below the water's surface are crucial to note. Of course, what's happening in the river is most influential to your success. Water temperature is an important element to consider when targeting summer steelhead. Throughout the course of the season, summer steelheading waters may undergo extensive shifts in temperature. The switch from cool to warm water—into the mid-50° range for many rivers—will increase the metabolic rate of these fish, making them much more aggressive. If the water is cooler, fish may take extra coaxing; likewise when the water surpasses the upper-50° level. Experimenting with various bait, drift bobber or lure types and sizes, the objective is to find what works. When you find what fish like in the respective water temperatures you're fishing, make a note of it.

Water clarity is another vital factor to keep track of. Whether the river is running transparent, or resembles that of an Alaskan glacial-fed stream, jot it down. The obvious effect of this is what size and color combinations of attractants you'll choose to match the conditions.

Water levels and turbulence are key elements to keep in mind and are worth observing. Checking local newspapers, website and information phone lines for up-to-date river levels provides a valued, objective reference through which important data can be documented. Ranges of turbidity are more subjective, but can be described in terms of feet or inches of visibility. If fishing below dams, or a series of dams, water levels and turbulence can have a major impact on fish activity and should be noted accordingly.

Distinguishing silt content, levels of visibility, and the presence of freshets are also key factors worth being mindful of. Due to erosion, storms or one of a number of human influences, silt content can vary within any river system. In addition to silt, vegetation, foliage and the process of photosynthesis in aquatic plant life can also hinder a river's level of visibility. If a river is running clear, heavy with silt or tea colored due to the release of elements in decaying vegetation, scribe it.

Freshets—freshly fallen rain, or snow that quickly melts—can also cloud a river due to runoff. But this surge of fresh water is what inspires fish to move upstream so rapidly. If you're fishing during a freshet, or shortly thereafter, note the number of fish you hook, you may be surprised at what you find.

Finally, weather conditions should be documented. Clarify all conditions that apply; the degree of cloud cover or clear skies, winds that might create chop and the direction from which it's blowing, temperature and even moon phases. Noting the time of day a fish was hooked and correlating that with current weather patterns is important information to retain.

The Human Factor

Given the level of human involvement in and around our river systems, it's imperative anglers take several of these factors into consideration when keeping records. The opening and closing of dam spillways can have a major influence on the rate at which fish travel, and keeping track of such activity helps anglers predict when fish will arrive at their favorite holes.

For example, on two particular rivers I like to fish, when the water flow is high, fish can make it to my honey holes in two-thirds the time it would take during what I consider to be a time of normal river flow. By keeping track of fish counts as they cross ladders on the systems you fish, and combining this with river level information, you can pinpoint, almost to the day, when those fish will show up. Patterning such fish movement is highly educational and surprisingly accurate.

Obtaining exact locations of where smolt are introduced into a river can be one of the most influential bits of information available. Fish and game offices have this information and much of it can be obtained off the Internet. Knowing precisely where smolts are dumped into a river is an event worth remembering, as three and four years later, these same fish will return as adults to the same location. The smell of these smolting grounds will also attract adult fish to the area that spring, offering good fishing.

Learning where hatchery trucks introduce steelhead smolt can be key to success. In coming years, adult fish will congregate at these sites, making for prime fishing.

If fishing a river on which fish are recycled, obtain recycling schedules from hatcheries conducting the activity. They will also share the number of fish being recycled and where they are being reintroduced. Knowing this information will allow you to assess when the bulk of the fish should arrive back in your favorite holes.

Record, Refinery & Reference

When returning home from a day on the river, it's worth a few minutes to jot down more complete notes while still fresh in mind. This can be done on paper or computer; even a calender for basic, quick referencing. The more thorough you are, the more your results on the river will prosper.

Of course, all efforts are useless unless you refer to what it is you've written. I like keeping records in chronological order, as these are simple to look back on. By pulling out a notebook, searching for data on the date I intend to go fishing in subsequent years, and referencing what's been recorded, it takes only minutes to anticipate what conditions may lie ahead, and better yet, what terminal gear to consider using.

In one of our favorite holes, Dad and I went seven consecutive years catching a limit on the same day, standing on the same rock, and using the same bait each time. Not until the river changed did the hole change, and the fish no longer use this site. But by referencing past records, we knew what to expect on that river, on that particular date. That is just one example of how record keeping can influence your fishing success.

Once you get into the habit of keeping records, you'll see how much it truly enhances the sport. It instills a level of pride, and by requiring you to be tuned in to so many factors relating to steelheading, it will increase the number of fish you catch through simple self-education.

Chapter 18
The Proper Release

$\mathcal{A}$ trip to the river found plenty of people catching fish. About 50% of the catch was made up of native, unclipped fish, meaning they had to be released. For the most part, anglers did well releasing their fish, but there were a few I observed who should be ashamed.

One gentleman netted a fish, dragged it ashore, and took a couple minutes to remove the hook and untangle the fish which was badly twisted in the net. Grabbing it by the gills, he hoisted it above his head to show his group of buddies who stood nearby. A streak of blood ran down the side facing me, having obviously ruptured a gill. Still holding the fish by the gills, he threw it back in the river, head first, with no effort whatsoever being made to revive it. The damage he inflicted was unnecessary and no doubt resulted in the death of a wild, adult fish heading to spawning grounds.

A few minutes later, this angler's buddy repeated a similar escapade. Had an anti-angler witnessed these—and a half-dozen other such acts I saw that morning—they would have had good reason to be upset; I was ticked by the wanton show of neglect.

Be it a fin-clipped steelhead or a wild fish, the time will come to release your catch. Properly releasing fish is an often overlooked element of the sport, yet one we as sportsmen and conservationists should practice with competence. A biologist once shared with me that 10% of summer steelhead released after being caught, die. This number can be greatly reduced by taking a few simple steps.

When handling a fish to be released, turning them on their back has a calming effect and reduces stress. But turn the fish upright prior to pumping it.

The ideal release begins the moment you set the hook. If fishing rivers with healthy native stock requiring release, I prefer going with 10- or even 12-pound mainline. The heavier line allows you to apply more pressure on the fish, landing it before it reaches the point of fatigue. The quicker a fish can be landed, the better its chance of survival.

If landing a fish you know is going to be released, avoid using a net. Nets remove the protective slime layer and some scales from steelhead, making them more susceptible to disease. Nets will also confine a fish, and this restricted movement greatly stresses them. With the fish in the water, simply reach down with a pair of pliers and remove the hook.

Prior to release, pumping a fish is often necessary to return it to a healthy state. If a steelhead is lethargic—that is if it lacks tail movement, power, and gill action—it needs to be pumped prior to the release. With one hand, grab the fish by the base of the tail. Support its belly with the other hand. Now gently begin moving, or pumping, the fish back and forth in the water.

In a slow, steady rhythm, pumping a fish is critical prior to release. This ensures adequate oxygen is being consumed under the fish's own power. A large percentage of fish can be saved if anglers take time to make the proper release.

Guard against vigorous, rapid movement when pumping—a slow, steady rhythm is what you're after. This action forces water over the gills, providing oxygen to the fish. Make certain the fish is in an upright position at all times, for their swim bladder, circulatory and nervous systems do not function to full capacity when on their sides or back.

Pumping a fish to full recovery may take several minutes. I've worked them as long as 15 minutes before setting them free. Don't be in a rush. Preserving the health and survival of that fish is the priority, not catching another one as soon as possible.

During the dog days of summer, when water temperatures reach a zenith, steelhead are easily deprived of oxygen in the course of a fight. During these periods, quickly landing a fish is critical, as is taking the time to revive it.

If snapping pictures of the fish you plan to release, do so close to the water surface. Avoid hoisting the catch into the boat, laying it on the floor, and removing the hooks. Hooks can be removed with the fish in the water, preferably with its head facing upstream. Wild fish should not be removed from the river, but during the pumping stages of revival, when they are partially out of the water, they can be positioned to take a quick photo without endangering their health.

When reviving a fish in fast water, ensure its head is pointing upstream at all times. Water running backwards over its gills depletes the quantity of oxygen that can be utilized. At the same time, avoid dragging a fish backwards through the water. Any time you move a steelhead in water, lead with the head by pushing from the base of the tail. This will maximize the amount of oxygen reaching the fish.

Tom Buller chose to keep this steelhead, but if you're intending to release a fish, slipping a finger under the gill plate is a sure way to kill it.

If, for some reason, you do have to lift a fish from the water that is targeted for release, never do so by inserting a finger beneath the gill plate. Not only does this increase the likelihood of ripping a gill, it removes valuable, protective slime, making them more susceptible to attacking bacteria.

The golden rule when releasing a steelhead: Never let a fish go until it's capable of escaping under its own power. Never force or toss a fish into the river. If released prematurely, the fish may go to the bottom, turn on its back and expire. If this happens, it's too late to save the fish.

By taking the time to properly revive and release a steelhead, not only are you practicing sound etiquette, you're promoting a strong fishery for future generations; as anglers, that is our responsibility.

Chapter 19
Hatchery & Recycling Programs

Thanks to the success of hatchery programs, they, in part, are the impetus behind this book. While many wild strains of steelhead are struggling, hatchery-run fish are picking up the slack. In fact, hatchery runs are solely responsible for an increased number of anglers taking to the rivers, be they seasoned veterans or newcomers to the sport.

Steelhead fishing prospects have come a long way in the past 20 years. In some rivers the cycle has shifted from all wild fish, to very few fish, to numerous hatchery-raised fish, and then to some hatchery fish mixed with wild fish. It's the hatchery-raised broods that are providing the most optimistic outlook for anglers. These fish are raised for one reason: To be caught by sportsmen in what is known as a put-and-take fishery.

The primary ingredient in the creation of a successful hatchery run lies in maintaining a disease-free program; not a simple task. This is why, for example, many of Oregon's hatcheries have turned to the South Santiam, near Sweet Home, to handle the fish. The South Santiam River Hatchery provides all the summer steelhead eggs for Willamette Valley programs. Biologists try to minimize the interaction of these summer steelhead with the indigenous run of wild winter steelhead in the South Santiam river. So, in early to mid-October, steelhead are no longer recycled back through the fishery, as is done from March through September.

The typical scenario in rearing hatchery fish starts with eyed eggs being placed in a facility that can house them until hatching. This may be done in several hatcheries, or, as is the case in Oregon, at a single hatchery located on the Deschutes River. The fingerlings are then taken to respective hatcheries involved in the summer steelhead program. From there, hatcheries introduce the smolts into the river.

Recycling summer steelhead from hatchery ponds to the river has dramatically enhanced the number of anglers on many streams.

With an annual fingerling supply numbering into the millions in western rivers, it's easy to see why the number of steelhead returns have held steady or increased in recent years.

From the beginning, these steelhead are reared for the sole purpose of being caught by sport fishers. This is where recycling the adults comes into play. Once the adult fish make their way into the rivers from whence they came as smolts, hatchery personnel and local volunteers may be kept busy for months on end.

Adult steelhead returning to hatchery holding ponds or collection areas at the foot of a dam, are placed in fish trucks, moved back downstream, and reintroduced into the river, a process referred to as recycling. During the capturing process within the hatcheries, some programs record the length of fish and place a tag at the base of their dorsal fin or make a notch in the caudal fin. Obtaining lengths helps biologists age the fish, while tags and marks allow them to monitor the number of times they return to the hatchery, or if they are caught by anglers.

By reporting every tagged fish you catch, (numbered or not), to the hatchery on whose system you caught it in, anglers can help biologists better understand steelhead movement. Be sure and tell them exactly when the fish was caught and precisely where on the river it was taken. This provides valuable data on how quickly fish move through a system, and if or when they are caught. In many rivers, steelhead make it over dams rather than ending up in hatchery holding ponds. If anglers are not turning in tags, officials are left to speculate whether the fish held in the river, made it over the dam, or were captured.

Some biologists are going so far as to implant radio tags in recycled steelhead. The active radio tag is a device with a tiny antenna that hangs from the corner of the mouth of the fish with the capsule end either slipped into the stomach through the mouth of a fish or surgically implanted. The radio tag

Inserting an active transponder into the gut of a steelhead, authorities are able to learn more about the mysterious ways in which these fish move.

emits a signal which can be monitored and tracked from up to a mile in fresh water, similar to big-game radio collaring.

What's being discovered boggles even the minds of trained professionals. While some fish recycled into a river may take three days to return to the holding pond from where they came, others from the same exact rerun effort may take weeks to arrive. What's more, the occasional fish will leave a system completely, entering other rivers, sometimes hundreds of miles away in another state.

The tagging of recycled fish is a valuable tool for monitoring fish migration and seasonal movements, all of which ultimately aid anglers. By keeping

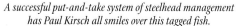

*A successful put-and-take system of steelhead management
has Paul Kirsch all smiles over this tagged fish.*

steelhead in the rivers for extended time periods, the odds of catching those fish greatly increases. Take a steelhead that enters a hatchery in April and is recycled to a lower point in the river to once again run the gauntlet of anglers; the chances of catching that fish improves 100%, versus its remaining in a holding pond all summer.

Now, imagine that fish making it through a mass of anglers three, four or five times. The result is that fish being recycled back into the river that many times allows anglers to test their skills on them over and over. Repeat that development with hundreds, even thousands, of fish and it's easy to see what an impact recycling efforts have in creating a quality summer steelhead fishery.

The South Santiam River is a prime example. During the 2001 season, they handled 6,600 fresh steelhead and about 6,300 recycled fish. They were so inundated with steelhead, officials were oftentimes making three to six runs with the fish truck a day, up to three times a week, to keep these fish in the river for anglers. They recycled a total of 11,350 fish downstream that season, keeping anglers on the river from April into October.

The allure of unraveling the unknown is one of the aspects that makes sport fishing so addictive. If we can better understand the movement of recycled summer steelhead on a micro scale, perhaps it may lead to larger discoveries on a global level which may help us preserve the sport we so zealously covet. Thanks to recycling efforts in many hatcheries—and the numerous volunteers that make it happen—measures are being taken to not only enhance summer steelhead fisheries, but to ensure that such runs exist for future generations.

Fisheries biologists on the cutting edge of steelhead management find valued insight that ultimately benefits anglers.

Chapter 20
Mounting Your Catch

You've just landed the steelhead of your dreams and would like to have it mounted. If it's a wild fish that must be released, what are your options? Be it a wild fish you are required to set free or a hatchery fish you want to turn loose, it can still be preserved in a mount.

If having a replica mount of your prized catch, getting an accurate length and girth measurement will help taxidermists match your fish.

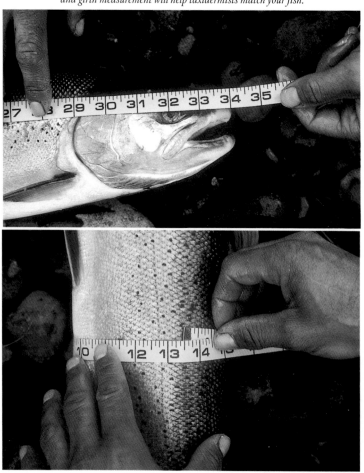

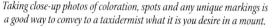
Following the guidelines for a proper release as outlined in Chapter 18, three quick steps can be taken that will allow you to accurately document and preserve the fish. While reviving a fish to be released, take a quick measurement of its length. Place a tape along side the fish while it's still in the water. Recording the nose-to-tail length assures an accurate replica can be attained.

The next measurement to take is the girth. Place a flexible tape around the fish, gently snugging it across the front edge of the dorsal fin and the widest part of the belly. Don't pull the tape too tight. You don't want the soft belly to become misshapen, throwing off the proportion of your mount.

The final step is to snap a few photos. These photos are not the ones of the angler posed with the catch, but rather close-ups of the fish. The objective is to capture spotting patterns and overall coloration of the fish. For these shots, focus on the best side of the fish, the one least blemished. At the same time, if there are any unique qualities you want preserved, say particular spotting or striping, make sure to get clear photos.

Taking close-up photos of coloration, spots and any unique markings is a good way to convey to a taxidermist what it is you desire in a mount.

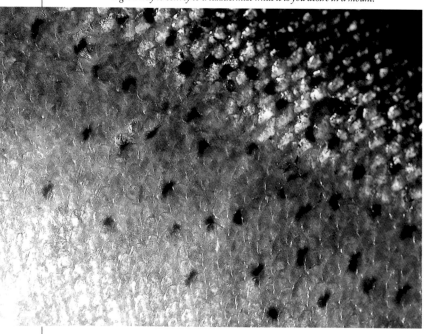

"Try getting photos of the head and overall color of the fish," advises Matt Yernatich of Artistic Anglers Taxidermy in Minnesota. "Steelhead coloration can vary from fish to fish, and capturing those traits is important if desiring a customized job. But if for some reason photos are not available, we can match a fish pretty close with a verbal description," offers Matt. In other words, if a camera is not on hand, or a fish gets away before measurements can be taken, it can still be mounted and the memories preserved.

When taking photos, get as close to the fish as possible without blurring the image. This allows you to document the characteristics you want highlighted in your mount. Photos snapped from too far away may not capture the details necessary to create an accurate mount. The better your documentation, the better the quality of the mount.

Submitting the photos and two measurements to a taxidermist is the next step. Artistic Anglers has mounted all of my fish, from Mexico to Alaska. They have also done the mounts for a few Cabela's stores.

While skin mounts are an option, be prepared to pay more. If going with a skin mount, note that discoloration due to oils in the skin of fish may occur over time. My dad has had a skin mount brooke trout remounted twice. The next time he's going to graphite.

Graphite replicas are economical and their durability lasts a lifetime. In addition, the finished product looks incredibly lifelike, as if the fish was just pulled from the river.

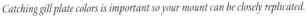

Catching gill plate colors is important so your mount can be closely replicated.

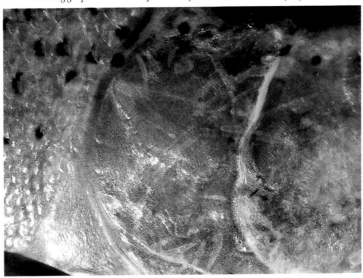

Chapter 21
Cleaning & Preparation

Obtaining the best-tasting steelhead begins the minute a fish is landed. Once photos have been taken, bleeding the fish and getting it in the shade or somewhere cool is critical. The cooler the fish can stay, the more firm the meat will be, thus maximizing its flavor.

Soon after the catch, bleed your fish by cutting the gills or ringing a cut around the underside of the base of the tail. Be aware that both methods release a great deal of blood and can make a mess in a river boat; it's best to do this over the water or in the fish box. It's vital to quickly remove the blood from a fish, thereby preventing bacteria from invading tissues which can taint the flavor of the meat.

If in a boat, fish boxes serve the purpose of storing the catch. If it's an extremely hot summer day, putting a bag or two of ice in the box, or carrying a cooler in which to store the fish is a good idea. Bank anglers can either kill the fish and hang it in a shaded tree or keep the fish in a cooler. Whatever you do, don't try to keep the fish alive by placing it on a stringer in the river.

Slicing the gills of a fish releases a great deal of blood, and is the first step in attaining quality meat.

Keeping big fish like steelhead and salmon alive on a stringer greatly stresses them. This heightened level of anxiety causes lactic acid to buildup within the muscle tissues of the fish, tarnishing the taste. Also, during hot summer months, the top layer of river water grows so warm, it often starts cooking the fish, or at least heating it to the point it becomes mushy and dull to the taste. For these reasons, avoid placing your catch on a stringer.

Anglers I know who catch and eat a large number of steelhead each season attest to the fact these fish eat better when quickly killed and bled, not kept alive. I agree. If you're bank fishing a river that allows the cleaning of fish, doing so is a good idea.

The ultimate goal should be to remove the blood and get the fish in a cool setting, void of direct sunlight, as quickly as possible. For this purpose, it's better to stash your fish on a shaded bank than in water touched by sunlight.

Slicing at the base of the tail, all the way to the bone, is another bleeding alternative.

Dressing Your Catch

The more quickly you can clean your catch, the better. Again, this prevents deteriorating organs, fluids and blood from contaminating the meat. Note that some rivers and states have regulations forbidding the removal of entrails from fish and tossing them into the river. If you clean your fish on such rivers, place the entrails in a garbage bag and discard when you get home; this will ensure you're not in violation. I save most of the heads and organs from fish to be used as crab bait.

It's also a good idea to remove the scales of your fish. This can be done with a knife, a strong garden hose, or, my favorite way, using six bottle caps nailed to a chunk of 2x4. Work against the scales, popping them off. This will prevent them from coming in contact with the meat during the butchering stages, thus fouling the taste with fish slime.

You can remove the head and entrails of a fish with three simple cuts. First, slit from the anus to the gills. Next, cut from beneath the pectoral fins, through the meat, and into the spine atop the back. Repeat this step on the opposite side. Now drive a thumb and forefinger into the eye sockets of the fish, snap the head toward the belly, breaking the spine, and remove the head and entrails all in one piece. The same can be done by leaving the head intact, but cutting out the gills. This is handy for carrying the fish or hanging it from a limb if bank fishing.

With the fish on its back, take your knife and slit the entire length of the kidney—that long purple organ lay-ing tight against the spine of a fish. Using the butt of the knife or a spoon, scrape the kidney out the front of the fish. Be certain to force all the blood from the veins inside the fish. This can be done by taking your knife and scraping over the veins, from the belly toward the spine. Thoroughly rinse the inside of the fish clean of blood and you're set for butchering.

Nailing bottle caps to a chunk of wood is the best scaling system the author has used.

Fillet O'Steelhead

Filleting a steelhead is easy and can be done when the fish is whole, or once it's been divided into chunks. I like to fillet my fish whole, then cut it into smaller portions. Some of the smaller rib bones will remain in the meat, but these are in a symmetrical line and easily removed once the fish is cooked.

When filleting a steelhead, keep the blade along the backbone and ribs at all times. This will yield the most amount of meat.

To fillet the fish whole, make a single cut the entire length of the spine. Ring a cut around the tail and remove the head as described above, if you haven't already done so. Using a long-bladed fillet knife, work snugly against the bone, cutting down toward the belly. Lay the fillet over as you go, exposing the bones, allowing you to salvage all the meat. Repeat the process on the opposite side and you have two complete halves of prime steelhead meat.

These halves are great for summer barbecues. If you wish to cut into smaller portions, it's easy from this point on.

Steelhead Steaks

If steelhead steaks are what you desire—complete with spine and rib bones attached—a sharp knife is needed. How the fish will be cooked determines the thickness of the steaks. Regardless of steak size, start by cutting through the skin, down to the spine on both sides of the fish. If you hit between vertebrates, getting through the spine is a cinch. If not, a sharp blade can be forced through the bones. An electric knife can greatly expedite preparing a fish in this manner.

When cutting the fish into steaks, take care in gently handling the meat so as not to damage the firmness. The firmer the meat, the better for cooking and the taste value.

With the meat clean of blood and debris, it's ready to be cooked or stored. If you're not going to cook the fish right away, it will keep in the refrigerator up to two days at 34° to 40°. Storing it for any longer will need to be done in a freezer. If freezing, I like wrapping my fish in a double layer of freezer paper to prevent freezer burn. Nonetheless, if looking to optimize flavor, don't keep the fish frozen more than three months at zero degrees or below. Keeping it in the freezer longer is fine for a fish that will be smoked.

There's no reason to rely on the local butcher to clean your fish for you. Cleaning and preparing your own catch is simple and a rewarding end to a successful day on the water.

Cutting fish into steaks is another way of preparing it for cooking.

Chapter 22
Into the Smoker

Smoked fish is a favorite among many people. This is a recipe I've refined over the years, and nearly everyone who tries it expresses the same sentiment; it's about the best they've tasted.

Take a gutted fish and remove the head, tail and all fins. With a long, sharp fillet knife, cut the fish into 4-inch cross sections. Each cut will go through the skin and backbone. Take each chunk and fillet both sides. The fillets are now ready to place in the brine.

In a large pot in which the fish will soak, mix 1 cup curing salt, 3/4 cup white sugar, 1/4 cup brown sugar, 3 teaspoons liquid smoke, and 3 teaspoons liquid garlic into 1 1/2 quarts of water. Stir the ingredients until fully dissolved. Add the desired quantity of black pepper and stir. If you're not a huge fan of black pepper, add only one tablespoon. If you like pepper, up to five tablespoons can be added. This is enough brine and ingredients to soak two large summer steelhead. If curing two fish at once, a crock serves as a good bowl. Its high sides accommodate the rise in water level.

The brine should be in a large bowl, to which the fish will be added. Place the fillets in the brine all skin-side facing up. To keep the meat from floating, place a slab of wood on top, weighted down by a rock or brick if necessary. Soak the fish for 3 1/2 hours. Too much time in the brine results in a salty product.

Cutting small fillets is a good way to prepare meat for the brine.

Remove the steaks and place them skin-side down on the smoker racks—larger pieces on bottom, smaller portions on top. Make sure the racks and drip pan are clean of all charred residue collected from previous use.

Remove the smoker's drip pan and allow two to four hours for the fish to air dry outside. Drying time depends on air circulation and humidity levels. Look for a glaze called the pellicle, to form over the meat to the point it's nearly dry to the touch.

Smoking time depends on several factors, including the type of smoker used, time of season, climate and amount of fish being processed. I'll freeze steelhead to be smoked year-round, but in doing so, make sure the fish is completely thawed prior to soaking in the brine. For years I've used Luhr Jensen's Little Chief Smokers. On hot summer days, the fish will smoke for seven hours. On cold winter days it smokes for 12 hours. If working in cold or cold and humid conditions, the cooking process may need to be completed in an oven at 250°. Convection ovens work particularly well for this.

In the winter, I prefer keeping the smoker in its original cardboard box or wrapped in an insulation blanket. If I'm craving a particularly strong smoke flavor, I'll burn two to six pans of chips during the smoking process. The flavor you desire determines what kind of wood chips you'll use.

With the fish cooked to desired firmness and dryness, remove the small bones and skin from the meat. It's now ready to eat.

If the meat is too moist, you can keep it cooking in the smoker or finish it off in the oven at 250°. If it's too dry, place the warm, de-boned, skin-free chunks in a large bowl and cover with plastic wrap. Moisture will condense on the plastic wrap. Occasionally tap the plastic wrap, dropping the moisture back onto the meat. The moisture will be reabsorbed, yielding succulent smoked fish. This is advised for those wanting to get the fish while it's still warm. When done, quickly place in the refrigerator, to preserve its shelf life.

*When removed from the brine, let the fish air dry on
the smoker racks until a gloss covers the surface.*

This recipe works on salmon and trout as well. Not only is this some of the best smoked fish you'll ever eat, but it makes a delectable dip.

Smoked Steelhead Dip

Work the smoked meat into tiny flakes, making certain all small bones have been removed. Taking one 8-ounce package of cream cheese (at room temperature) and 1/2 cup of sour cream or mayonnaise, mix the two together until smooth. Add 1 teaspoon of Worcestershire sauce, 1/2 teaspoon garlic powder and 1/2 teaspoon of onion powder and mix thoroughly. Gently stir in 1 1/2 cups flaked smoked steelhead and you're set.

The dip can be served right away, or cooled in the refrigerator for two hours, shaped into a ball and rolled in crushed almonds or walnuts for a decorative presentation. Refrigerate the unused portions for future use.

Sandwich Spread

One of my favorite sandwiches is made from steelhead spread. It's a great way of preparing leftovers from the barbecue, broiler or frying pan. You can also do the same with smoked salmon.

Break the cooked steelhead into small flakes, making sure no bones remain. Gently mix in 2 cups flaked steelhead, 3/4 cup mayonnaise, 1/2 cup finely chopped celery, 1/2 teaspoon salt, 1/4 cup finely chopped onion (optional), 1/4 cup sweet pickle relish and a dash of black pepper. Thoroughly mixed, the spread is ready to eat. Keep unused portions refrigerated until ready to serve.

Smoked fish is not only delectable by itself, but as sandwich spread and dip as well.

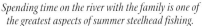
Chapter 23
Conclusion

When it comes to fishing for summer steelhead, the rewards that arise are unique to the heart of the individual pursing them. But it's the diversity of positive feedback that makes summer steelheading so treasured. Perhaps it's those hot summer days that draw you to the river, when the sun beating on your back helps remove you from the chaos of work. Maybe it's the challenge of trying to outwit, on a regular basis, one of the continent's greatest fish. Chasing summer steelhead is this and much more.

*Spending time on the river with the family is one of
the greatest aspects of summer steelhead fishing.*

For me, it sparks fond boyhood memories of being on the water with my dad. I can close my eyes and smell the river, see the dry grasses whipping in the wind and taste marshmallows cooking over an open campfire. Chasing lizards around camp was something I loved, but grew away from as steelhead began luring me to the stream. Now it's my boys who chase the lizards around the tent; I can't wait until they discover just how wonderful the world of steelhead fishing truly is.

While vivid memories are indelibly etched in my mind, it's the creation of fresh experiences that keep me going. Exploring new waters, trying new tactical approaches and meeting people who share my passion for the sport is what makes it enjoyable for me now.

Braxton Haugen exploring steelhead on the riverbank.

These fish keep my wheels turning, always testing my knowledge and often proving me wrong. It's when I think I have them figured out, and come home empty handed, that are the most humbling times. As a lifelong outdoorsman, I should know better. Few things found in nature are a guarantee, and this is especially true when it comes to catching steelhead.

But it's the ease of access and the high rate of success that hooks people on summer steelhead fishing. Given improved runs in recent years, more anglers are taking up the sport. I've also chatted with many veterans who had hung up their rods due to a lack of fish; now the dust is being removed and those wise feet are heading to rivers. The good ole days are back.

Talking with fishermen, elder or otherwise, can shed light on any angler's base of knowledge. I actually learn a good bit each summer chatting with local high school kids while on the river. There are some hard-core lads who hit the river every day, and though they

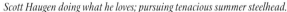
may not realize it, are developing skills that have the potential for turning them into top-notch steelheaders. Talking with these kids is a great way to get them to communicate what they've learned, and really gets them fired up about fishing. It's these kids who hold the future of steelhead fishing in their hands.

It is my wish that the words appearing in this book have been beneficial and that you will become a more complete summer steelhead angler, having read it. And while there are some incredibly gifted steelhead anglers out there, no one knows it all, and the "experts" are the first to admit this. By keeping an open mind and possessing a willingness to learn and apply new ideas, only then are we on our way to becoming well-rounded anglers. Open your mind, open your heart, and let summer steelhead take you into a world of fishing unlike any other.

Scott Haugen doing what he loves; pursuing tenacious summer steelhead.

Appendix

Action Optics
P.O. Box 2999
Ketchum, ID 83340
www.actionoptics.com

Artistic Angler Taxidermy
5289 Rice Lake Road
Duluth, MN 55803
(218) 721-4900
Attn. Matt Yernatich

Atlas-Mike's Bait, Inc.
P.O. Box 608
Fort Atkinson, WI 53538
(920) 563-2046

Beau Mac Enterprises
3280 B St. N.W., #V
Auburn, WA 98001
(253) 939-8607

**Berkley Fishing
Line/Pure Fishing**
1900 18th Street
Spirit Lake, IA 51360

Cabela's
One Cabela Drive
Sidney, NE 69160
1-800-237-4444
www.cabelas.com

Catcher Company
5285 N.E. Elam Young Parkway
Suite B700
Hillsboro, OR 97124
(503) 648-2643

Coleman Company, Inc.
P.O. Box 2931
Wichita, KS 67201-2931
www.coleman.com

Columbia Sportswear
14375 NW Science Park Drive
Portland, OR 97229
1-800-547-8066
www.columbia.com

Danner USA
18550 NE Riverside Parkway
Portland, OR 97230-4975
503-251-1110
www.danner.com

Do-It Lure & Sinker Molds
501 N. State St.
Denver, CO 50062
(319) 984-6055
www.do-itmolds.com

Flambeau Outdoors
P.O. Box 97
Middlefield, OH 44062
(440) 632-1631
www.flambeau.com

Gamakatsu USA Inc.
(West US)
P.O. Box 1797
Tacoma, WA 98401
(East US)
3900 Kennesaw 75 Parkway, Suite 14
Kennesaw, GA 30144
www.gamakatsu.com

LaCrosse Footwear
18550 N.E. Riverside Parkway
Portland, OR 97230
1-800-828-6987
www.lacrossefootwear.com

Luhr Jensen & Sons
P.O. Box 297
Hood River, OR 97031
(541) 386-3811
www.luhr-jensen.com

Mack's Lure, Inc.
11779 Highway 2
Leavenworth, WA 98826
(509) 548-5241
www.mackslure.com

P-Line
G. Pucci & Son's, Inc.
P.O. Box 140
Brisbane, CA 94005
www.p-line.com
1-800-537-2394

Pro-Cure Bait Scents
P.O. Box 7077
Salem, OR 97303
1-800-776-2873
www.pro-cure.com

Brett Stuart
24/7 Guide Service
P.O. Box 125
Thurston, OR 97482
1-888-761-5203
e-mail: fishnfamily@juno.com
www.fish24-7.com

Yakima Bait Company
P.O. Box 310
Granger, WA 98932
(509) 854-1311
www.yakimabait.com

More Excellent Fishing Books!

SPOON FISHING FOR STEELHEAD
Bill Herzog

One of the most effective ways to hook steelhead (and salmon) is with a spoon. Bill Herzog covers spoon fishing techniques for the full year, going into finishes, sizes, weights, shapes, water temperature differences, winter and summer fish differences, commercial and custom spoons, spoon parts suppliers, and reading water. Scores of color photos enhance the book, along with many line drawings, graphs and illustrations. 8 1/2 x 11 inches, 64 pages.

SB: $14.95   **ISBN: 1-878175-30-0**

COLOR GUIDE TO STEELHEAD DRIFT FISHING
Bill Herzog

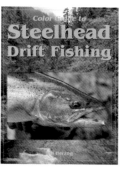

Each year nearly 1,000,000 steelhead are hooked in North America and the great majority of these fish are hooked using drift fishing techniques. This lavishly illustrated, all-color guide is the "bible" if you want to get in on the action. Written by one of America's greatest drift fishermen, you will learn the techniques that can guarantee your entry into the 10% of the anglers who hook 90% of the steelhead. This is a heavy-duty graduate course! 8 1/2 x 11 inches, 80 pages.

SB: $16.95   **ISBN: 1-878175-59-9**

SPINNER FISHING FOR STEELHEAD, SALMON & TROUT
Jed Davis

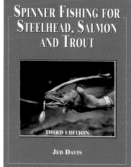

The "bible" for spinner fishing and the most in-depth, non-fly-fishing book ever written about steelhead and their habits. Information on how to make spinners is complete, including how to assemble, obtain parts, even how to silver plate. The fishing techniques, lure, line color and size selection, and reading fish-holding water sections are excellent. 8 1/2 x 11 inches, 97 pages.

SB: $19.95   **ISBN: 0-936608-40-4**

FLOAT FISHING FOR STEELHEAD
Techniques & Tackle
Dave Vedder

"Float fishing for winter or summer steelhead is terribly productive. It is uncomplicated and the hook-set is almost always effective as opposed to drift fishing. Float fishing is the easiest (no snags), most effective way to hook steelhead. Vedder's all-color book explains all the methodology and tackle choices. This is the wave of the future." —Frank W. Amato 5 1/2 x 8 1/2 inches, 64 pages.

SB: $15.95   **ISBN: 1-57188-039-9**

Ask for these books at your local fishing or book store or order from:
1-800-541-9498 (8 to 5 P.S.T.) • www.amatobooks.com
Frank Amato Publications, Inc.
P.O. Box 82112 • Portland, Oregon 97282